Bedfor
Within Livi

C000129016

WITHIN LIVING MEMORY SERIES

Other Counties in this series include:

Hertfordshire   Somerset
Northamptonshire   Staffordshire
Shropshire   Surrey

Bedfordshire Within Living Memory

Compiled by the Bedfordshire
Federation of Women's Institutes from notes
sent by Institutes in the County

Published jointly by
Countryside Books, Newbury
and BFWI, Bedford

First Published 1992
© Bedfordshire Federation of Women's Institutes 1992

COUNTRYSIDE BOOKS
3 Catherine Road
Newbury, Berkshire

ISBN 1 85306 200 6

Cover illustration: The cover photograph was taken
at Duloe c. 1944 and has been kindly supplied by
Mrs F. E. Hawkins, who was then in the Land Army.

Cover Design by Mon Mohan

Produced through MRM Associates Ltd, Reading
Phototypeset by The Midlands Book Typesetting Company,
Loughborough.
Printed in England by J.W. Arrowsmith Ltd, Bristol.

Contents

Acknowledgements

Bedfordshire Federation of Women's Institutes would like to thank all W.I. members who supplied material for this project through their local Institutes.

Unfortunately we were not able to include extracts from every submission; to do so would have meant some dupli cation of content, and of course we had to take into account the total amount of space available in the book.

But all the contributions, without exception, were of value: deciding the shape and content of the book. We are grateful for them all.

Finally, special thanks goes to Mrs P Challenger for her lovely sketches.

Eileen Parker
Co-ordinator

Foreword

When the older generation take a trip down memory lane it is often hard to stop the flow – that is until you want to record their reminiscences! With the passing of the years memories fade, so gentle persuasion was used to compile this book wherein the reader will find an abundance of local memories from the past few decades that are still within living memory.

'Give me the good old days' no longer rings true for me since I have heard how people in the rural areas had to work so hard to survive.

Children would leave school as soon as the statutory age was reached to start full-time work, mostly locally due to the lack of public transport. Many girls worked at home without a wage or went into service, which meant living away. Women's lives were vastly different from today with none of our modern conveniences and often a shortage of money therefore it was essential for the housewife to be a skilful manager to make ends meet.

The working day for men was much longer than today, often starting the day with a long walk or cycle ride to his job particularly if employed as an agricultural worker.

The rich harvest of memories to treasure and the many interesting facts make the compilation of this book both fascinating and rewarding. Grateful thanks must go to Bedfordshire W.I. members and their friends for the work entailed in collecting all the information.

Within Living Memory is an important contribution to charting the social history of more recent times in our locality.

Shirley Nash
County Chairman

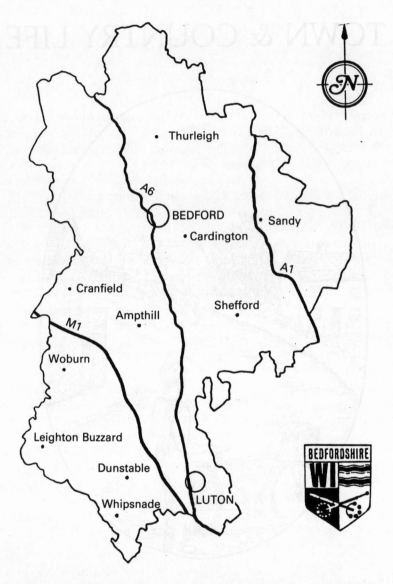

The County of Bedfordshire

TOWN & COUNTRY LIFE

SOME TOWNS AND VILLAGES REMEMBERED

Saturday afternoon shopping in Luton Market and going home by open-topped bus; Milton Ernest in the days before it was bisected by the A6; a part of Dunstable now gone for ever; rural Flitwick in the early 1950s – these are just a few of the vivid memories recalled of Bedfordshire towns and villages as they were.

LUTON MEMORIES

'Saturday afternoon shopping in Luton was always a family event. Into town on the bus, and a first call was to a very special sweet shop, next door to the Town Hall. It was called "The Black Boy" and the window was full of beribboned boxes of chocolates, or baskets or silver dishes, all with different types of chocolates; people would just stand to admire the window display. Mother always had a quarter of chocolate nougat whilst my sister and I had a two ounce bar of something or other, which we had to save for Sunday. Sunday was always special – Sunday school, a special tea, all together for chapel in the evening, me wearing my gaiters in the winter – they were leather and squeaked, then home to eat our sweets and fruit and a game before bed.

But back to the shopping. The Market was the place to make for. It was quite an Aladdin's cave. In through the swing doors in Cheapside (opposite Chapel Street), past Climpsons the florists and into the large glass-domed hall. Endless stalls and little shops on the side selling dresses, materials and slippers, and there was the glove man – only leather gloves, no plastic – china, hardware, it was all there. Then through to the fruit market and into an open air part which could also be approached from Market Hill – where Barclays Bank is today. Here were more fruit and veg stalls, one which only sold celery at four pence, six pence and ten pence per head, then the fish market, but best of all was the Candy Man. He had two large sugar boilers in which he mixed his candy or cough sweet mixture, and the candy would come out a pale coffee colour which he would knead and knobble and then swing it up on a large hook and pull it, and again, and again. Finally it would emerge in a long strip with brown stripes down the centre, to be put through the machine to come out as humbugs. The mouth watering smells, the gas lamps, the jostle, with men and women shouting their wares, made shopping fun – not a chore like today . . . but then I was only ten.

Home on the open top of a double decker bus is another memory which makes me smile. As we approached the railway bridge near to Mill Street, the conductor would call up the stairs "Mind your heads please" and adults would bend forward to avoid their hat or hair being caught up, but I took no chances and crouched on the floor!'

'I was born and spent my early years in the Hightown district of Luton. War was declared when I was in my sixth year and Luton, being famous for its hat industry, had a lot of the tradespeople drafted for call up or to work in the factories to supply ammunitions.

To own a car, you were someone special; Shanks's pony or the bus were the usual forms of transport. Workers on their way to work had the streets echoing with their blakied heels, which were repaired at home. Ration books were issued to enable us all to have a fair share of food for our daily meal, but even so queues were the order of the day, though these gave opportunity to catch up on all the latest gossip. Another queue we waited in for hours, or so it seemed, was for the cinema. The glamour of American film stars in glorious technicolour, transported us from our black and white existence of the war years.

Living next to a large park I considered myself lucky, but the street games were for the street. There was hardly any traffic to interfere with our fun: hopscotch, the old favourite, skipping alone or with a group, whip and top, the top chalked different colours to create patterns as it spun. Marbles and cigarette cards all came out in their season. Some games we only speak of now. The lamp in the street, usually gas, had a bar just under the light and careful tying of cotton left to hang would have ladies passing beneath hastily wiping their faces, to our delight hiding out of sight. Cotton, again, tied from one letter box to another had a lot of very annoyed neighbours all answering their doors to face one another. The nights were very dark due to the blackout. No light was allowed to show after dark in case enemy aircraft could see us from the sky. This made hide and seek very exciting and lively around the block and in passage-ways.

The tradespeople, such as the baker with his hot bread, the Co-op milkman, the coalman, and the brewery, all had their beautiful horses to pull the carts. They knew every stop and where their feed bags were fitted, impatient stamps with hooves soon brought attention. I can remember calling my father, "Come quickly with bucket and shovel before the neighbours get there". My dad's garden was his pride and joy. My friend's grandfather was a blacksmith at the bottom of North Street. He made the horseshoes and fitted them as we watched. I was always so fearful that it was hurting the horse but they did not seem to mind.

Richmond Hill was one of the sights for the smoke burners in Luton; these belched out thick black smoke to cover the town and we all tried to keep indoors when these were in action.

Sunday mornings was when I would supplement my pocket money, taking a neighbour's baby out for a walk. The bigger the pram the more esteem among my friends.

Barton Cutting was still white chalk and a cycle ride to Barton Springs with a picnic was nearly a day out. We gathered wild violets for a sick teacher, but these were received with a very strained "thank you" as familiarity was not encouraged. A lot of our school friends were evacuees from London, some whole families moved and settled in Luton.

Teachers' and policemen's words were law; it did not occur to us to question them, any cheek would mean another reprimand from Mum. All the people seemed very close. The war brought us together; old people looked old and did not worry about it, life itself was too important. We always had it drummed into us

13

to give up our seat on a bus to a lady or elderly person.

LMS trains passing through or making a stop at Luton would let off their steam and smoke giving us an obstacle to pass through, over the bridge above, before the train had passed. Chesty children, and looking back it is a wonder any of us survived, were taken for a walk around the gas works to inhale the sulphurous fumes to clear our chests.

Despite all, we had a very happy childhood.'

MILTON ERNEST

'Milton Ernest has the doubtful distinction of being bisected by a busy trunk road, the A6, which at the turn of the century was only a rough track along which animals were driven to market. There are now only two residents who were born in the first decade of this century, and who can remember the pre motor car era which was also without electricity, piped water, main drainage and gas supplies.

In those days, apart from the few large "gentlemen's" residences, houses were 17th century cottages, thatched and built of stone brought down the river from Pavenham, of which only a few remain. Gardens were cultivated mainly for vegetables to feed the family, as well as allotments on the outskirts of the village.

Men earned their living mainly from agricultural work, about ten shillings a week, apart from those engaged in one of the 30 or so businesses or trades in the village, now only a handful. Milton Ernest was fortunate in having the Oakley Hunt kennels in the village, creating jobs not found in other villages. On long dark evenings, the family would be encouraged to help in making rugs from strips of old material, in which one of the bright red huntsman's jackets was much prized in contrast to the usual dull colours of clothing. All the family were alive to collecting and selling anything legally available, such as men or youngsters collecting ploughshares from the fields, mushrooms or acorns; hedgerow flowers by children and the women who also picked blackberries. One lady used to pick enough blackberries to sell at three farthings a pound each autumn, to buy new shoes for her children to wear on Sundays, when all the family appeared in their best clothes, reserved for Sundays.

But it was not all work and there was a great sense of family in the village with most people supporting the seasonal events such as a Spring Fair, the annual Flower Show causing keen rivalry, a large Harvest Festival supper in one of the big farm or estate barns, as well as celebration of National events.

In addition, most villages had active football and cricket teams which attracted support for both home and away fixtures. Most of the home games were played in Milton Ernest Hall park, owned by the Starey family for some years, at which time the Scout movement also received great support from Capt Starey who was County Commisioner. At one stage, Lord and Lady Ampthill were in residence, including years of the First World War, during which two of the young Royal Princes who lived at the Hall were to be seen hugely enjoying themselves racing round the park on their bicycles.

The house and grounds were put to a very different use during the Second World War as the nerve centre of USAF Communications HQ, among whose residents was the famous band leader Glenn Miller.

Village charities still exist which were set up during the very hard conditions prevailing during the 18th and 19th centuries. Even in these days of greater affluence, and the Welfare State, they are still appreciated on occasions.'

DOWNRIGHT DUNSTABLE

'I thought we lived in a medieval castle with iron-leaded "church" windows, shuttered too, and a white wooden bell-tower beyond. It was really Victorian Gothic, the Ashton Boys' Schoolhouse in 1915!

My happy childhood home in Dunstable has gone now and with it the boys' tops, hoops, roller skates and cigarette collections. They sat at iron-clad desks where open inkpots froze in their wells in winter, and where "The fear of the Lord is the beginning of wisdom" was carved above the biggest fireplace. No tidy lawns and flowerbeds now, but I can still hear, echoing from the windows, "Be present at our table Lord", boys' voices rising in Grace before Meat and Thanks when reassembling after it. At the adjoining girls' school white pinafores were "de rigeur". The school bell rang so punctually at 8.45 am that men set their watches by it.

My first memory of an event beyond home and garden is in a field. I sit on a wet form at a trestle table bordered by other children and am given a paper bag containing cakes and a doughnut. It followed the Peace Procession at the end of the First World War. The Ashton Schools had entered as their decorated horse and cart, "The British Empire – Peace"!

Miss Scott taught the youngest boys in my father's school and on fine Saturday afternoons would take me for enormous walks, my seven-year-old legs carrying me across the Downs to Whipsnade Common for blackberries, or to Sewell for beloved wild flowers. But coming home along that interminable chalk cutting one afternoon I was excited to see a horse and trap – the only traffic on the Watling Street – draw to a halt, its driver inviting us to a lift. The ride was even more special than accompanying the old boy who collected Sunday papers from Church Street station with his horse. His next door family possessed a "Sundays only" parlour where the Bible stood ever-open on its reading desk. Coal was delivered, rubbish collected, and ploughing done by horses, while I dug energetically in the garden, told that a secret passage once led from the Priory to the Litany field beyond the Ladies Lodge. Wind from the Downs was keen: "Someone has left the gate open at Dunstable", Luton people said. But we youngsters relished ice cream from the crossroad cart, if we had a penny to buy one!

Opposite, the great priory church was the inspiration of my childhood, its sturdy Norman pillars and air of timelessness gave me a sense of history and a love of the Church of England that have lasted till now. From the "Ashton" came its choirboys, "Dunstable larks".

Told at the age of 12 that I must leave dear "Downright Dunstable" I cried myself to sleep. The future, I felt then, could never be quite as good.'

CLIFTON

'Our village of Clifton before 1960 was truly rural. Nearly all the men worked on the local farms, which grew "farm" crops of wheat, barley, oats, vegetables, potatoes, brussels sprouts, cauliflowers and beans, all termed now as old fashioned!

Our farmers bred and raised dairy cows and pigs (some hundreds in this village – known as the "pig village"), and also poultry was a good earner, the eggs being collected by a local firm, graded and sold to the larger town shops.

The dairy farmers delivered milk around the village, when customers had to put out their own jugs to be

filled. Clifton had its own farrier, who had lived in Clifton all his life; he could also mend implements should they break down, ploughshares were a speciality. The ploughs were horse-drawn of course. There was a rake and hurdle maker also (he lived next to the farrier), in fact when his wife needed a rake and there were none in the store she made her own!

The women used to do a lot of straw plaiting, in fact the building is still there, only now known as Straw Plaits.

There is always a May Day at school and a Christmas concert. Now they also have an outing to something of interest. In our day we walked the village or one of our farms and if given a glass of ginger beer (made in the village) it was so wonderful, even though "they" used to say the water came from the pond opposite.

There was good bus transport every hour from the village to Hitchin and Bedford, and the train stopped at Shefford station approximately one and a half miles away, again to Hitchin and Bedford. We used to catch the 8am train to Bedford for school, home at 6.15! Now there are no trains or stations, it's a sad world.

We did have an annual fair in Clifton, the first weekend in September. It had everything we thought, (even water squirts and confetti) certainly it was always packed with people. In fact the fair still comes each year.

There were five village shops and six local pubs, so all in all there was no need to go out of the village. There was also the village bakery and shoe mender, in fact you name it, the village had it. Those were the days.'

STUDHAM

'I came to live in Studham when I was about seven years old, a long time ago. Of course there was no form of transport, you had to walk everywhere, or go by pony cart.

There were very few houses in the village, but everyone knew each other and helped one another. There were a few of what we called Big Houses, three public houses, and several farms. There were no houses at all in any of the woods. We used to go play in any of the woods and I spent a great deal of time in them.

After a long time electricity was laid on, so of course, it made a great difference to us all. Before, our only means of lighting was by candles or oil lamps, and as for cooking, that was by fire, we had no cookers in those days.

The first council houses were built when I was about ten years old, and by that time there were a few cars about and we even had a bus service once a week.

When I got married, we still had no electric and we had to cook by fire. I remember my first iron, it was a flat iron, the only type available. The only drinking water we had was got from a well in the centre of the village, but oh what lovely water it was. When our rain water butts ran dry our husbands fetched us water so that we could do our washing, otherwise we had nothing, not even sinks.

The children were very safe in those days, you didn't have to worry about them at all, as they played with one another and enjoyed what few pleasures they had. We had lots of snow in those days and were often cut off as the roads were blocked and very little transport was available.

The men who worked in the towns often had to walk. They used the hedges as a guide when it snowed. On the whole we really enjoyed life as we were used to each other. There were no houses at all in Holywell, Oldhill Wood, or Swannells Wood. There were hardly any houses on the way to Dunstable. To go on a school trip meant going by a farm cart. We would go as far as

Bricket Wood or Ashridge Park. These were our only treats and how we enjoyed them.'

FLITWICK

'As a young married woman in the early 1950s, my first home was in Flitwick. We could only get a bus from Bedford to Ampthill and then we walked. The cottage was in Dunstable Road and it was supposed to have belonged to the painter Sylvester Stannard at one time. It was for sale for £600; the adjoining cottage was for sale with a sitting tenant and we bought the two for £800. Our cottage had electricity and cold water but no lavatory. When I went next door to collect Miss Bunker's two shillings and sixpence a week rent, I was amazed. There was no electricity and just a tap under the stairs. There were several Stannard pictures on the walls, if it had been light enough to see them. Each would be worth thousands today; I remember Miss Bunker saying she wouldn't sell even if someone offered her £50! Her kitchen was shadowed by a barn that housed the bucket lavatory. When we had our cottage modernised, we offered to have hers done – she refused.

I had come from London and could hardly believe how rural Flitwick was then. One day, I went to catch a bus for Bedford: I waited ages until someone took pity on me and told me there were only buses on Wednesdays and Saturdays, Bedford market days. If you went out of the back of our cottage in spring and walked towards Flitwick Woods, the fields were yellow with cowslips and here and there orchis flowers. When I went to church, I didn't wear a hat, and someone took me aside afterwards

21

and told me how shocked she was. After that, I always wore one.'

LIFE ON THE COUNTRY ESTATE

Many villages in Bedfordshire were part of large estates, the local landowner having a great influence on the lives of men and women, both at work and in leisure time. In general, the relationship this created within a community is remembered with pleasure.

CHILDHOOD AT WOBURN

'My mother often spoke of the days when, as a small child, she lived in a tenant's cottage on the Duke of Bedford's estate at Woburn (always pronounced Wooburn). It was around 1898 and her father was a painter and decorator. He later died from lead poisoning. Sometimes my mother and her younger sister, Queenie, would be sent to the dairy with a can for milk. They had to cross the park where the ostriches roamed freely. If the children dropped their ball the birds would seize upon it and swallow it. They would watch the round outline going down the length of the neck until it disappeared. Mother dreaded and feared the ostriches, but said they never to her knowledge attacked anyone.

The staff were treated very kindly by the Duke, and Christmas was the highlight of the year when all the tenants were given a large joint of venison and a sack of coal. Everyone was most distressed to hear of the tragic episode when the Duchess was missing in her aeroplane.

When my mother left school the family moved to Luton where there was plenty of work in the hat trade. She spoke with regret about leaving Woburn, and how she missed all the beautiful surroundings and peaceful country life. A few years later she was desperately ill with TB and was sent to a sanatorium in Yorkshire. It must have been indicative of life at that time when she said that her months at the "San" were the happiest days she had ever had.'

'I was only nine when my father became pilot to Mary, Duchess of Bedford and we moved to Froxfield House, by the Park gates. After this, life became more and more exciting. The Park was private then but we were able to enjoy its 3,500 acres. With the deer and the bison all around us we played and walked in it every day, with the occasional but often eventful trip to visit our governess near the dairy.

My father, with the Duchess, flew a Percival Gull and a Tiger Moth, making frequent trips to Africa. I recall one occasion when they returned with bullet holes in the aircraft. Monkeys occupy the airstrip now, at Woburn. Then, there was the wonderful birthday party the Duchess gave us in the Riding School – since demolished – and among the presents, a suitcase full of sweets.

I had leg trouble around this time and it was the

Duchess who attended to my treatment. This was when I became her ornithological pupil, taking me round all the bird hides on the estate. She was very deaf and would say "You listen to the birdsong, then we can find the birds." Once when she was away, I wrote to tell her I had seen a snowy owl. "Impossible!" she wrote back, "Try never to lose your accuracy in bird-watching or you'll never be believed." Of course it was a barn owl! Together we kept books of the sightings of all the birds. I have them still and bird-study remains one of my hobbies today.

One memorable occasion was going to stay at Ensleigh, their lovely home in Devon. With my maid, we left in the ducal Rolls Royce to stay overnight at Belgrave Square, then on to Devon next day. My father always flew down with the Duchess. I remember one morning coming downstairs for breakfast, dressed in a bright yellow jumper and black check skirt. "Good morning, scrambled egg" said the Duke! With watching and recording bird sightings everyday, it was a wonderful visit.

Christmas was an exciting time. Before the carol singing the Duchess lowered an enormous cracker, full of presents, from the Abbey windows. Lunch was slightly awesome with a footman standing behind each chair, and facing us was the huge array of cutlery on the table. We had to be sure we used the right piece first! After lunch we were sent out to the maze, never to appear again.

Every day at Woburn was enjoyed to the full, living in such beautiful surroundings, with all the birds and wild life, watching the aircraft come and go, looking after our pet rabbits and my guinea pig, Bunty, the visits with an artist friend to the Sculpture Gallery, and drawing the figures.

The fate of the Flying Duchess is now history. She was a Fairy Godmother to me and I have wonderful childhood memories of Woburn.'

MILTON ERNEST HALL

'An uncle of mine was a tenant of Lord Ampthill, who lived at Milton Ernest Hall before the First World War. Sometimes he would send a groom to fetch my mother and my aunt to swim with Prince George (the late Duke of Kent) and Prince John (who died young) because they were both petrified of water and it was thought that the sight of two small girls swimming so well would encourage them.'

TINGRITH MANOR

'The village was mainly made up from six families. At that time it was quite common to have large families; I had five sisters and three brothers and we all lived with Mum and Dad in a two up, two down cottage, with an outside toilet. No running water or bathroom.

All the houses and farms were owned by the Manor. All the men worked in the gardens, parklands and farms. The grounds were kept beautifully. There was a gravel path which ran from East Lodge to Eversholt Road (about a mile long), one from the back of the church to West Lodge and opposite the school another path went through a spinney of shrubs to the front of the Manor. Opposite Toddington Lane there was a gate and through this gate was a wooden bridge over the brook and then a cinder path which led to the back of the Manor. This entrance was used by the workers as this was where their cleaning and store sheds were, also the kitchen was situated at the back of the house.

The parkland stretched from one lodge to the other; no animals were kept on this land, two lakes were at the bottom. Between the two lakes was a large mound and inside this was a brick well that was used to store ice from the lakes to keep meat etc. It was kept locked by a gate on the front. (This was before refrigerators had been invented.)

The manor itself was a beautiful house and most of the rooms had wood panelling. It was set in a cobbled courtyard on three sides, with the stables at the back.

The owners at the time were the Hubbards, who were connected with the Luton hat industry. At Christmas there was a large tree put up in the village hall with a present for every child in the village and a special tea party laid on. It was the highlight of the year.

People in the village got their water from a tap in the road, this was fed from a natural spring at the top of a hill. It was collected in buckets and was used for every need; rain water was also collected in water butts outside the houses. There were also two wells in the village.'

THE BURGOYNES OF SUTTON

'The last Sir John Burgoyne died in 1921 marking the end of an era at Sutton, and is remembered by many of the older locals. His reputation for regimental order was known throughout the village and even today people talk of how it was expected of them to raise their caps on meeting any member of the family, and allowing the family coach to pass unhindered was essential, even if it meant a cart full of potatoes being tediously pulled up onto the verge, usually resulting in some of its load being spilt. The children were required to respect the family who governed their and their families' lives.

Church attendance was a must for all children, and any child causing a disturbance or talking during the service, was marked on the back by the butler of the big house, using a piece of chalk on a long cane. The offending child, on leaving the church, would receive a sharp crack on his backside by Sir John, this being the punishment for his crime!

The school house was built in 1870 by the Burgoyne family to provide education for children from four to 14. It consisted of two classrooms with open fires in each room, and the toilets were limited to two buckets in the cloakroom. The school had both boys and girls but at playtime they were required to be segregated. Children were required to develop their reading and writing skills using sand trays initially, and later progressed to slate. Sir John Burgoyne would visit the school once a month to sign the register and the children were invited, once a year in the summer, to the house for a tea party on the lawn, and for Christmas they would attend a party at the rectory.

Many of the local people lived a quiet rural life. Sutton supplied its occupants with requirements such as a blacksmith, a village pond, common land for grazing and a local carpenter, who acted as the village undertaker. Men and women both worked the land as tenant farmers or employees to the estate. Like many large houses, Sutton Park boasted a kitchen garden of about three acres, tended by the father of Mr Tom Britton, a resident of Sutton all his life, who at the age of 89 has a sharp wit and a good memory. He recalls tales told by his parents of a local witch with the ability to see in the dark and to turn herself into wild animals when it suited her! It is said that once, being chased by dogs, she ran across the fields at the back of the village shop, where she lived, reaching home just in time to take her human form from that of a horse.

The First World War brought soldiers to Sutton who were billeted in some of the local cottages. As a military family, the Burgoynes were keen to help, and the Land Army was also placed on farms in Sutton, although they actually lodged in Potton. Some of the local families took in evacuees.

Farming was the main industry in Sutton, and it was farming methods that helped to discover some of its older history. On Portobello Farm Stone Age relics were found and also remains of animals such as mammoths and tigers. It was shortly after the war that a local farmer who had his cows on part of the park lands, discovered what is thought to be part of a tunnel leading to the church from the park house; not the house we see today, but one of the two houses that preceded it. The discovery was made when the land collapsed, causing one of the cows to fall in. The cow was recovered with nothing more than a shock, and the rest of the village a little better informed. Many had heard of the existence of such a tunnel by means of a local story which is still enjoyed today – it is that of two Royalists escaping from occupying Roundheads, down the tunnel to what they thought to be safety, only to be greeted by Roundheads – and their imminent demise!

Sutton has changed greatly over the past century. In 1938, after the death of the last Lady Burgoyne, the estate was divided up and sold. Many of the tenant farmers bought their land and made some of the cottages tied cottages. People moved further afield and, sadly, some of the remaining thatched cottages fell into disrepair. However, Sutton still enjoys echoes of its historic past with the help of the ancient pack-horse bridge and an imposing rectory.'

AN ESTATE VILLAGE

'Until 1951 Bletsoe was an estate village, being part of the Melchbourne estate of St Johns of Bletso. The Castle was not lived in by the family but was rented out. However, all villagers employed on the estate or who lived in one of the estate cottages, were expected to curtsey or touch the forelock as their employer went by. All were expected to attend church on Sundays and Good Friday. If the farm workers went to church on Good Friday morning they would get the rest of the day off – if they were not churchgoers, they would work all day.'

'Tempsford between the two world wars was a quiet little village. Most of it belonged to the Tempsford estate and the majority of the men were employed either on the estate or on the various farms in the village. Several were also employed on the railway as linesmen, signalmen or porters. Quite a few trains stopped at the station in those days and it was quite easy to get to London or Peterborough, or any towns in between.

There were two shops in Station Road, a butcher's and a general store. In Church End there was one small shop, also the post office. Also in Station Road were the Methodist chapel, two pubs and the blacksmith's forge, which was a very popular spot with the children, who would watch Mr Wilson and his son shaping the hot metal and heating their irons in the furnace before reshoeing one of the farmhorses. The boys would also get Mr Wilson to make them iron hoops which they trundled along the road to school. The school was on the main road and we would spin our tops along there too. There was not a lot of traffic in those days.

Mrs Stuart owned Tempsford Estate and lived in Tempsford Hall. She was the widow of Colonel Stuart. Their only son, Esme, was killed in 1916 on the Somme. After Mrs Stuart died in 1932, the Wynne family came into the estate and came to live at the Hall. Owen Wynne (who now owns the estate) was born shortly after the family came to Tempsford. An oak tree was planted the morning he was born, in the front drive to the south of the house.

Mr Ladds kept the post office. He was also the church sexton and gravedigger etc. Several evenings a week he would deliver bread in the village, walking with his barrow and lantern from Church End to the station, calling at each pub for refreshment. The village lads would seize this opportunity to hide his barrow in some dark gateway.

At the station the goods yard was kept busy. Dairy farmers from nearby villages brought milk in churns by lorry to be put on the train for London. Sugar beet was also sent by goods train and coal was brought by train from the North to be unloaded by the local coal merchant.

In 1938 Tempsford Hall was leased by Dr Hales, who

turned it into a Health Clinic where the rich and famous would come to be restored to health and beauty.

Tempsford village is now divided by the busy A1. The school is closed, the shop, post office, butcher's, blacksmith and railway station are no more. Tempsford Hall is an office block.'

SIGHTS AND SOUNDS OF EVERYDAY LIFE

If you were walking down a town or village street between the wars, what could you expect to see? Horses, certainly, either on their way to the blacksmith or to work or stable, but there were also plenty of human figures in the scene. The lamplighter appeared at dawn and dusk, and the muffin man, the knife grinder, or the rag and bone man might be there, crying their wares. There would also be the tradesmen and craftsmen, such as the blacksmith, the baker and the local milkman, not to mention the amenities of the inn and the village hall.

THE STATE OF THE ROADS

'At about the time of the First World War, the roads around Sharnbrook were just mud and these were scraped from the centre into the gutters. There was a large puddle in the road between Thompson's Corner and the bottom of Kennel Hill and in the winter this made a superb slide.

Later on, when mother worked at Stoke Mills as a secretary in the 1920s, she biked each day and the roads consisted of large granites which were rolled in, but as they were large they came out, making cycling dangerous. Everyone knew, even in the dark, where the holes were.'

SENDING HOME THE HORSES

'I often used to visit the blacksmith on my way home from school at Biddenham, to watch the farm horses being shoed. When the village men finished their farm work for the day, they would let their horses into the field by the pond, and if working at Manor Farm would open a gate and let them through. If, however, they were working at the other end of the village, they would release them and let them find their own way back. The horses would charge through the village, which frightened me on my way home from school, especially if caught by the high wall bordering what is now Manor Hospital.

I remember fetching milk from the farmer straight from the cow, and calling at the pub for vinegar for mother to pickle vegetables; also avoiding the hundreds of frogs when they were crossing from one pond to another to mate.'

MUFFIN MEN AND LAMPLIGHTERS

'The earliest recollections of street traders in Dunstable are of about 80 years ago, when they included muffin men ringing their bells, rag and bone men, knife grinders, and, of course, gipsies selling wooden clothes pegs, paper flowers, lavender, lace and pins. There were also men who bought rabbit skins. Street singers were common with their musical instruments, walking down the centre of the road collecting pennies. Each night the lamplighter would go along the road lighting the gas lamps.'

'At Kempston at about the time of the First World War, the street lamps were gas and every evening Mr Carding the lamplighter went round on a bike carrying a ladder on his shoulder. He would put it up to the lamp post, climb it and light the gas.

Practically every street had a shop in it. There were six bakers and every day except Sunday they would come round with their carts selling bread. The milkman came every morning with his float, which had a big churn on it. If you wanted milk you took your jug to him and he measured it out, either half or one pint. The coalman came round every week and if you heard his call, "Coal", you went out and told him if you wanted any. The rag and bone man also came, calling "Ragbone", and if you took him anything (he also took jamjars) he gave you a paper windmill on a stick.'

THE TOWN CRIER

'Doris has vivid memories as a child in the early years of the century of Charlie Irons, the Town Crier. He was employed by the Luton Council and was to be seen regularly around the town, principally in George Street in the area of the old Corn Exchange on Market

Hill, ringing his bell and shouting out the news of the day – local news, anything taking place around the town and news from the Town Council. He was a very familiar figure in the town and people flocked round to hear him. He could be seen three or four times a week ringing his bell, his main route being George Street and Bute Street. He wore a dark uniform and a tall hat and Doris even has memories of him in a red cloak!'

KNOWING EVERYONE

'The main difference in village life as I grew up in the 1940s and 1950s was that we were very much a community. We had a police station and we knew all the policemen who we would shout a greeting to on our way to school. We knew the station master and the porters, the signalmen, the doctor and the district nurse, the coalman, the vicar and all their families plus everybody else who lived in the village. We spoke to everybody! I found this disadvantageous as a child as one step out of line and your parents were bound to hear about it! But it must have been good from a disciplinary point of view.'

THE BAKER

'The baker was a key figure in the village. Many cottage homes did not have good ovens and Sunday morning saw a steady stream of people carrying their meat in a tin to the bakehouse with the Yorkshire pudding mix in a can. The people went to church or chapel whilst the baker took care of the meal of the week. This was collected after the service and carried home wrapped in a cloth. Many people also took pastries and cakes throughout the week to be baked at the bakehouse.'

'Many villagers at Stevington had their Sunday roast lunch cooked at the bakehouse. The puddings would be lined up on the counter waiting to be cooked, with the joints waiting in tins with lard on top and covered with a cloth. At twelve noon all would be ready and we would watch the baker with his long paddle-like implements take the tins out of the cavernous depths of the oven. Often a wedding cake would appear in the bakehouse window, to display the baker's art and the fairyland spectacle of white iced tiers of cake with a silver vase and flowers on top.'

'It was towards the end of the 19th century when my late grandfather William Kember came to Leighton Buzzard and established his bakery business at No 4 High Street. His speciality in those days was coconut slices and they, as the saying goes, went like hot cakes, the price being a penny or a halfpenny according to size. My grandfather was either the first or second businessman to make his own ice cream in this town.

As time passed and my grandfather neared retirement, it was agreed that my father, Walter Kember, being the eldest son, would come to Leighton Buzzard and carry on the business. Consequently my parents and we five children arrived in the town and made the bakery our home. We all in turn had to help make the ice cream, by turning the handle of the barrel in which the ice cream container had been placed, plus breaking up the ice with a pick axe and placing it round the ice cream container.'

'The bakehouse at Milton Ernest, now a private residence, was one of the oldest in the country, parts of the building dating back to the 15th century. The ovens were originally heated by faggots, but later rebuilt and heated by coke.

Customers were from all the surrounding villages, the only means of transport being a horse-drawn, open box-cart. Each village had a special day for delivery, Saturday being Thurleigh's day. At 4pm Mr Newell, the baker, would leave his yard, loaded with bread. He took with him a small boy to help with the running about as some houses were in fields approached by muddy cart tracks, but winter, summer, rain or shine, the bread was delivered. He would arrive back in the bakehouse yard at about 10.30pm. The baker, however, still had a couple of hours work to do before he could take his well-earned rest.

The bakehouse was an unofficial meeting place for the villagers for not only was bread baked there, but cakes and dinners also. This was indeed a boon as many old cottages had poor ovens. Every Sunday morning dozens of people would hurry down the street with joints of meat in baking tins and batter in jugs or around the meat, and at dinner time would collect the meat which was done to a turn and surrounded by Yorkshire pudding. The charge for this was about two pence.

Miss Jane Newell, affectionately known as Jenny, often accompanied her father on his rounds, and on the death of her parents and brother took over the business. Jenny delivered bread in the village on foot, taken round in a barrow made of wickerwork. It had two large wheels and long, curved handles. Every day except Sunday, Jenny's familiar figure could be seen as she called from door to door. She had a buxom figure and cheerful rosy face. She wore black high boots, a long skirt and large white apron, with her brown hair in a bun, under a broad-brimmed hat.

Each Saturday twelve twopenny loaves would be placed in a special box in the church. This had been a bequest by Suzannah Rolt in 1726, "To the Poor of this Parish Forever". This practice stopped when the bakehouse closed in 1956.'

'I was the last tenant in the house adjoining the bakehouse at Colesden – the bakery has now been demolished. Mr Clay used to do the baking of the bread when I lived there in the 1940s. He was known as the Midnight Baker and would still be out on his rounds at ten o'clock at night, when he still had to deliver to Wilden.'

THE MILKMAN

'My earliest recollection is that of being photographed next to a milk churn, which was much bigger than myself, and being told that when I grew up I would be able to spin it across the dairy floor – just like my father.

My father had his first dairy at the back of a shop in Elstow Road, Bedford – opposite Brookhurst Igranic in 1930, and then moved to more purpose-built premises in Ampthill Road where he was known as "Tuckers Dairies" and finally in 1948 to Maulden at Snowhill.

In the London Road area he established – in modern jargon – his first customer base, which in those days consisted mainly of good hard-working families living on council estates. His brother used to rush, twice a day, breakfast and afternoon tea to the big houses in Shakespeare and Ashburnham Roads and "doff his cap", but as they say "one man's meat is another man's poison".

Father had 14 horse-drawn rounds that went round the town – and I enjoyed feeding them. The horses were of a special interest to my sister who, seven years older than myself, enjoyed riding. I recall quite vividly on one occasion when the horse bolted and broke the shafts of the milk float, with father and son coming to grief in the middle of Ampthill Road! Time has not changed much as the traffic goes even slower now in Ampthill Road!

The worst part of being a milkman's son was the unearthly hours that were kept. When I was around ten or eleven years of age onwards, during school holidays you had to be up at 3.30am to get to Maulden by 4am to load up and start the first delivery at around 4.30am. We often would not make the last delivery till 2–3pm in the afternoon. The reason being that father was a great one for chatting to the ladies and we would have to stop at certain places and houses to consume tea, biscuits and cake. I was always given orders; two here, three there, gold top or double cream, and when you had gone up the Brache at Maulden, to a long row of terraced houses to which you mostly delivered to the back door, only to be told "none today son" or they wanted twice as much, it was hard to put on a bright smile and "look lively" when you felt far from lively and were only looking forward to bed.

I suppose looking back it did me no harm to be up early, but when I was allowed a choice, to my father's disappointment, I never wanted to deliver another milk bottle!'

'At Thurleigh milk was taken straight from the cows, often still warm, to the door. Even in those days hygiene was strictly observed. Usually someone had the copper boiling so that all milk utensils were scrupulously washed with strong hot soda water. Yet diseases and TB were rife, not necessarily because of dirty conditions but because until the early 1930s no one seemed to know that cows themselves were sufferers and carriers.'

THE WINDMILL

'I can remember coming out of school on a windy day at Stevington and seeing the sails of the windmill gyrating; climbing the stairs and feeling the whole structure shake and throb, accompanied by the heavy flap of the sail-cloths; holding fingers under the soft textured flour as it ran down the chutes, still warm from the power of the grinding stones.'

AT THE VILLAGE INN

'In the late 1940s there were three pubs in the village of Roxton. At The Pear Tree, where the buses stopped on the Bedford Road, the ale was fetched from the cellar and one sat on high backed bench seats. As 14 year olds in 1945 we would sing in the choir on Sunday morning and then go and have half a shandy in the Pear Tree passage. I recall in the 1950s a rather posh car driver coming into the bar to have a drink. The pub was mainly used by farmworkers but apparently this gentleman had been to Newmarket races and had a good day out. He said to the landlord, "Drinks on me, all round the house!" Well, we nearly all soon had a refill, bar one chap, known to us lads as "Sipper" – he would make half a pint of shandy last two hours. The gentleman said to Sipper, "Will you have a drink?" "No," said Sipper, "but I will take one home for my sister."

The Chequers is also closed now and there is just one pub left, The Royal Oak on the crossroads. It always had a steady trade and here too, the landlord had to walk to the cellar to fetch ale. Mr Fred Ball, one landlord, he was a character in his own right. On Fridays we lads would often visit all three pubs in an evening. This particular Friday we had come from The Pear Tree and it was nearly closing time. I asked Fred for a drink, offering a pound note, but "No," he said, "I haven't got any change, go back and drink where you have been all night!"

Aside the Royal Oak stood an onion loft, one of three in the village. It was not unusual to see bicycles outside "The Oak" with hoes tied to the crossbars; often these men had been "up Rood Field" where they had a piece of ground to grow vegetables. One fellow I know spent most evenings on his ground out of the way of his Missus. Most households had their own back garden for vegetables and many kept a few poultry for eggs and fattened a fowl up for Christmas.'

'One of my most vivid childhood memories was listening to my mother recall her childhood in the early 20th century. As a child she lived in the Brewery Tap public house which was situated by the roundabout of Park Square, Luton. She was the youngest of five children, three boys and two girls. At this time the circus used to come to town and parade through George Street up to Park Square. My mother would sit upstairs at a window and watch the procession and can remember that a man used to tap on the window. As she was only four at the time this frightened her as she used to think he was a giant; of course, as she got older she realised that the man was on stilts. All the animals were in the parade with clowns and jugglers performing as they walked along.

Another one of my mother's favourite stories was how she used to go to stay with her friend called "Cissy" at The Plough situated on the Corn Exchange. They were fortunate enough to have a maid and also had a pulley system on the outside of the building which went from the window of the upstairs lounge to outside the back door. The poor maid was summoned by ringing a bell and then had to send the breakfast or anything else they fancied up on the pulley. As you can imagine the maid was put through the mill by these two young girls who had such power.

Her father was quite a strict man who had good and bad moods so at an early age she learnt to tread carefully if it was a bad day – equally on a good day she was invited into the bar and entertained the customers by tap dancing on the counter. On these occasions she was rewarded by a half pint of bitter as her bedtime drink, other times she went to bed empty handed. Unfortunately her father died in 1915 when she was just ten so the family had to move from the Brewery Tap as in those days a woman was not allowed to be a licensee of a public house.'

'When the Second World War started there were four public houses in Little Staughton village but one was burned down in mysterious circumstances and two were demolished to make way for a wartime airfield, which left The Crown at Green End to carry on alone. This old fashioned inn stood back from the road down a narrow lane and looked like a quaint old thatched cottage. Inside you found low ceilings with rough hewn beams and an inglenook fireplace, at night lighting was by paraffin lamps.

Being the only pub it was very busy with service personnel from the airfield, who joined the locals playing darts and skittles and drinking beer. The Crown was only a beerhouse having no licence for serving spirits, beer being drawn straight from the barrel and carried through to the tap room.

The landlord William (Billy) Lumbers used to entertain the customers by playing his violin accompanied by a lady on the piano, all joining in a good old sing-song. Playing darts could be very hazardous, the darts often hitting the low beams instead of the board, and tall players had to bend their knees when throwing to avoid mishaps.'

THE VILLAGE HALL AND READING ROOM

'From the humble origin of two thatched cottages, the Millbrook parish reading room was created in the latter half of the 19th century by the owner, the Duke of

Bedford. When he sold his Millbrook properties it was purchased by the village, refurbished and given the grand title of Millbrook Village Hall.

Opening their stocking on Christmas morning, the cottage children would have been over the moon to have received the type of present that used to be given at village Christmas parties. How brightly its white pebble-dash must have shone with importance at the opening ceremony of the Parish Room as it was then called. One of the first events to be held there was a magic lantern show. All events seemed to be patronized by most people in the village whether it was for the church, chapel or whatever. The village in those days was a close knit community with everyone joining in together. The village socials were the real highlight of events – no wallflowers were permitted there and usually something amusing would happen to create the village talking-point for the next few days. Dancing classes, whist drives, sausage and mash suppers were only a few of the events that took place. Casting one's mind back, the art of self entertainment has definitely been lost since those times.

In 1929 Millbrook WI was formed, meeting in the Parish Room once a month with the Hon Romola Russell as President. This proved to be a boon as the WI purchased a piano. Previously the piano was conveyed from the school for any event and then taken back for school next morning. Crockery was also bought by the WI and both that and the piano were gladly lent to any other event so the days of "take your own plate, cup and saucer" were over. Now the village hall has a modern fitted kitchen and gone are the days of those big cast iron kettles propped up on the fire to boil. What a contrast from the old school piano with its candles in holders to the flashing disco lights of today.'

'Stevington had a reading room and institute on the corner of Silver Street and Court Lane. Upstairs there was a billiard table and socials were also held there, while downstairs in the front was the reading room with books, and cards were played. However, when the players started to gamble, in the late 1930s, it had to be closed!'

THE BLACKSMITH

'There were always horses queuing up to be shod in Church Road in Stevington, with the old men who looked after them sitting in a long row waiting and children standing watching the shoeing on their way to and from school. The shop closed in the early 1960s.'

'The blacksmith at Thurleigh kept the horses well shod and also made at the forge requirements such as gate fasteners, hinges and wrought ironwork.'

'Sometimes on wet days when you couldn't work in the fields we had to take the horses down to the village blacksmith's at Cople to be shod, and if you weren't early there would be perhaps five or six more horses there so you would be nearly all day. I used to like watching them being shod. The blacksmith was getting on a bit in years as he used to shoe mules and horses in the First World War. The blacksmith's shop was opposite the pub and he lived next door; his name was Fred Wheeler and he was very fond of his beer. He always had a bottle in the shop

44

and when it was empty he'd say to me "Go and fetch me a bottle of beer, boy" and I'd have to put the bottle under my coat so that his wife didn't see it.

One day when there were a few horses to be shod I thought I would have a try at taking some of the old shoes off and I got on fairly well. I did that a few times, then I tried trimming their hooves up a bit and after a while I was getting on alright so when the blacksmith had fitted the shoes and put the nails in, he used to leave it to me to drive them in. Then I would break the nail, just leaving a little bit to turn over after you had run the rasp round the hoof. You could then bend the nails over and rasp them round and they were finished. Sometimes we put a little oil on with a brush to make the hooves look nice. I think if we had kept horses a few more years I would have been able to shoe them myself. There isn't a blacksmith's shop there any more, it is a garage and filling station, but the pub is still across the road.

Sometimes we would take our horses to the blacksmith at Ickwell Green. It was very pretty there with trees around the shop – it always reminded me of the poem about under the spreading chestnut tree. The shop was on the corner of the green and from there you had a good view of the cricket pitch and the maypole. Mr Reeks was the blacksmith and his son Jed used to help with the shoeing or pointing up the harrow tines or any other odd job. The thing I remember most about them was that they both stuttered. I have been there sometimes all day and they were never in a hurry and would talk a lot about cricket as the family used to look after the pitch on the green. When Mr Reeks was shoeing a horse and there was a fly about, making the horses a bit fidgety, he

45

wouldn't start shoeing until he had killed it. I have seen it many a time.'

MARKET DAY

'Leighton Buzzard is a market town and has always, as far as I can remember, had a street market on a Tuesday and Saturday. Tuesday is still "Tiddley Tuesday", due to the pubs staying open all day for the farmers. There has been a cattle market for very many years, before which animals were tethered in the street and I can still remember the animals on Fat Stock Day, before the 1940s, being in the Church Square.

It was a common sight to see the bargees in the town when they stopped over in Leighton. They were a colourful sight in the barges on the Grand Union Canal. Several of these families settled in the town when the barges were not used so much.'

THE GIPSY CARAVAN

'In the 1940s I was asked to tea by the old gipsy woman in her caravan at Bromham. It was beautiful outside and in, with shiny brasses everywhere, so cosy and clean. I went to see her as often as possible. I was sometimes allowed to sit on one of the horses when it was taken to the brook to drink.'

FIRE!

'One Monday morning in 1949 a chimney caught fire in Silver Street, Stevington and a spark, swept along by the high wind, caught the thatch of a neighbouring cottage. The resulting fire destroyed eight cottages. A call came through to J.P. White's in Bedford where quite a few Stevington men worked, to return home immediately and the radio reported that a whole street had burned down. The press came in force, and fought one another to use the phone box.

The fire was fought by practically everyone in the village, led by Rev Whittle, with the men operating stirrup pumps on the rooftops and the women struggling to carry pails of water from the pond and the village pumps. They could do little against the strength of the wind, however, and it took a mere half-hour for the cottages to burn down.'

CHURCH AND CHAPEL

When Sunday was a special day of the week, set apart from the other six days of hard toil, going to church or chapel and, for the children Sunday school, was simply a part of life. The Sunday school treat or outing was an eagerly awaited event in the lives of children, and adults, who rarely had the opportunity to travel far – a first glimpse of the sea would be a heady delight.

SUNDAYS

'My mother always attended Stevington church. I attended Sunday school in the afternoon, and my mother would go again to church in the evening. I remember she used to take the playing cards with her so that nobody could play on the Sabbath while she was away – no knitting, sewing, lace making etc. Dad was allowed to play ludo with the smaller children. Mum always wore a hat when going to church.

In the summer after church, we would meet my mother outside the church and go for a walk by the river, ending up at a nearby public house, where my mother would have a glass of "porter" and the children would have a packet of biscuits. A great treat on a Sunday evening.'

'Luton at the turn of the century was very small, being situated in a hollow surrounded by hills and beautiful countryside, and walking was a popular pastime of the day. On Sundays whole families and young people went out to meet and make friends, dressed up in their Sunday best clothes. They walked out to Wardown Park in their hundreds, bearing in mind that Wardown Park was some way out of town in lovely countryside. The band played every Sunday and deckchairs were set out and could be hired for a penny or so for sitting out and listening to the music, and picnics were taken. What is now the museum was in those days used as a cafe – the front of the house being opened as a tea room with chairs and tables set outside for refreshments. Different bands played each Sunday, the Beds & Herts Territorial Band, the Salvation Army Band and the Red Cross Band. There was no sport at that time – it was simply a beautiful park to walk in and listen to the band and meet people.'

'On Sundays no toys were allowed in my mother's home

at Kempston. All were put away Saturday night. She was allowed a picture Bible but nothing else, and the emphasis was on Hell and what would happen if you were not good. Even a button lost was not sewn on again until after Sunday. During the First World War her mother, who was a great knitter, started knitting socks for soldiers on Sundays. Very sinful, it was thought.'

GOING TO CHURCH AND CHAPEL

'When people got married in Bletsoe in the early days, the church was much bigger and they were married at the proper altar at the end of the chancel. Nowadays, that part isn't used and the chancel has been bricked off underneath the tower, so today there is a small altar right in the middle of the church. In the old days, practically everyone went to church. There was a great tradition of good singing in Bletsoe even though it was such a small village and all the children were encouraged to be in the choir. They got used to being part of the church and continued to go when they were older.

Before the war, Mrs Polly Green played the organ. She used to get all dressed up in what we called her "crushed strawberry", which was a suit she wore for church. With it she always wore the same hat, but the trimming changed according to the seasons. On her feet she wore those black button shoes that do up over the instep. When she wore them down on one side, she changed them over on to the opposite foot, so they had a new lease of life. One of the young boys always had to pump the organ; it was before they converted it to electric. Sometimes their minds wandered and in the middle of a hymn, the music died away. Mrs Green would shout "Wind, wind . . ." and the hymn would continue.'

'There were three churches in Kempston at the beginning of the century – the parish church with a vicar, and St John's and St Stephen's in Spring Road which had curates. I attended St Stephen's as I lived in the Barracks for the first ten years of my life. It was a tin church but a very busy one.

Sunday morning was very exciting and the Bedford Road would be lined with people, some from Bedford, waiting to see the troops going to St John's church (this was the garrison church) headed by the band, all in their red uniforms. After they came back the public were allowed in to watch the band playing on the square.'

'My brother and I were brought up by our grandparents, who being very strict Baptists made sure we always attended the Little Staughton Baptist chapel Sunday school in the morning, also the afternoon service, and again for the evening service. We used to walk the one and a half mile round trip each time from the age of six and seven.

Sadly this lovely chapel building had to be demolished during the Second World War as a result of the roof being wrecked by a loaded bomber taking off from the wartime airfield. The new chapel, though very nice, can never in my estimation replace our old chapel when I remember the lovely times we had. The tiny Sunday school building still remains where we also held social evenings.

Whitsun was a big day in the chapel calender when we kept our Chapel Anniversary. For about six weeks before the big day special hymns would be practised on Thursday and Sunday evenings after the evening service, and there was also a special anthem. There was great excitement looking forward to the celebrations. One reason was that we all had new clothes including hats, and we all wanted to see who looked the best. The chapel was full, including the large gallery. People came from many surrounding villages, and we had a special preacher also for the following Wednesday when we had the Anniversary tea in the chapel schoolroom. After tea we had great fun and games in the chapel field. Mr Usher, a deacon of the chapel, would bring sweets and scatter them in the field and we all scattered too, I can tell you, to see who could find the most. Then it was back to the chapel at 7pm to sing again to finish another Anniversary.

In January we had the Sunday school tea and prize giving. We all had to perform recitations and sing special hymns, but best of all we all looked forward to the prizes which were books, very nice books too. There were special prizes for the boy and girl with the best attendance record of the year. We all went home at the end of the evening very happy and pleased with ourselves with our prizes and an orange. Sadly these days are gone but the prize giving still takes place.

The chapel outings were great fun; we either went to the seaside or to Wickstead Park. These outings were very exciting because when I was a child over 60 years ago this was the only opportunity to travel right away from the village. There was little sleep the night before an early start at 7am for our journey.'

SUNDAY SCHOOL

'We had one outing a year at my chapel. I remember one occasion (in the early 1920s) going, I think, to Ashridge –

51

quite a long way in those days. We arrived early morning and waited for the "charabanc" to arrive. It was a large bus with no fixed roof, only a large sort of cover to pull over if it rained. There were steps along the side of the vehicle and once you were in and seated, little doors with brass handles were closed for safety. I can't remember whether it rained that day but I shall never forget that "charabanc" and the good time we had.'

'One of my most cherished memories is of my mother's face as she watched with a mixture of pride and anxiety as I performed in the annual Sunday school concerts. These events were arranged to raise funds for the chapel. As there was no permanent platform in the rather bleak school hall, a temporary stage was erected using the tops of trestle tables. The audience sat on hard wooden forms.

My first solo appearance, at the age of four, was to recite a little poem about a spider. No-one had told me that at the end, a large spider with wire legs would be lowered from a beam above my head. My unrehearsed reaction to this earned me an instant reputation as a talented actress!

There was always a musical number with the little boys dressed as elves, small bells jingling on their caps and brown stockings. We little girls preened ourselves in fairy dresses made of crepe paper, generously trimmed with tinsel, as were our wands. How the stage creaked under our feet as we performed lumbering dances. Ballet shoes were unknown in our workaday twenties' world.

How we loved our first encounters with the world of show business. As a result I became hopelessly and eternally stage struck!'

'Highlights of the year were usually fetes, chapel teas and outings. Sunday school outings gave adults and children alike something to look forward to. Wickstead Park was a favourite, though occasionally there was the rarity of a trip to the seaside. It was a big event and needed organisation. A train was guaranteed from Sharnbrook station. Every child took pennies to Sunday school for months beforehand, and Mums, Dads, Aunties, Uncles, Granny and Grandad all joined in. Many people in the first half of the century had never seen the sea or imagined what it could be like, so these trips were a sensation.'

'There was a building at the back of St Stephen's in Kempston which was called the Institute, where we held our Sunday school and where on other days there were social evenings, whist drives and dances. We had a Sunday school treat, all three Kempston churches together, in the summer. We all walked together (it seemed a long way) to the chosen site and we had to take our own mugs so we had them hanging round our necks on a piece of string or ribbon. The tea was made in a big boiler and always tasted of disinfectant. We had various races and other games and scrabbling for sweets, then we had to walk home – very tired.'

'According to my parents I started Sunday school at the Potton Congregational chapel in 1930. Although I have no recollection of the beginning of my Sunday school days, I remember clearly four special events.

Prize Giving Day was held in January. We all met in the central hall attached to the chapel. Trestle tables were laden with sandwiches, jellies and cakes. Mr Barringer, the Superintendent, would hide pennies around the room. No child ever went home without finding one. An impromptu concert was followed by the prize giving. Children were given a Bible, a hymn book or a suitable story book by a special visitor. Those who had put in a full attendance won first prize. We applauded each child but by the time the third prizes were awarded many children were too busy looking at their own prizes to clap. Before going home each child received an orange.

The Sunday school Anniversary took place in June. New hymns had been learnt which included solos and duets. Poems were included in the programme. We girls looked forward to this event as we all had a new hat and dress which we did not wear until the afternoon service. The children were supported by their families and friends. A story was told by the Minister, then children and adults joined in the final hymn. Whether it was the excitement of the new dress or nerves at having to recite, Sunday dinner on Anniversary day was not enjoyed. Sunday tea was another matter!

For our Sunday school outing we were taken on Mr Bartle's buses to either Wickstead Park or the seaside. We had great fun at the park as there was much to do – swings, slides, a water-chute, rowing on the lake or riding on the miniature railway which took us round the lake and through a tunnel. Tea was provided in a large building near the rose garden. If the day was to be spent at the seaside, east coast resorts were chosen. For many children it was the only time they saw the sea as few fathers had paid holidays before the war.

Finally the October Concert was held to raise money. Two iron cylinder stoves heated the room. The evening performance included everyone from the primary class to the teachers. Nursery rhymes were always popular, costumes being made out of crepe paper. I remember being Bo-Peep, wearing my blue bridesmaid's dress and holding a crook. The oldest scholars contributed choruses, action songs and recitations. "Ten Little Nigger Boys" was a favourite, performed with blackened faces! If any child had an individual talent such as piano playing, tap or ballet dancing, this would be included. The teachers' sketch was the grand finale. This was a special night looked forward to by the people of Potton as well as chapel folk.'

'On Sundays at Salford and Hulcote we attended Sunday school at 10am and 2.30pm. There were two classes in the morning. Miss Bennet, who also cleaned the church, had the ones under eleven in the church near the font. Others who had reached the grand age of eleven plus were seated with the rector in the vestry. He had a way of talking to children making them feel on the same level as adults, at these morning sessions. In the afternoon we had a half hour children's service with hymns, prayers and a little talk.

A looked-for Sunday afternoon was when a baby was brought to be christened. We felt part of the family, leaning round in our seats and singing "In Token That Thou Shalt Not Fear Christ's Crucified To Own", after the sign was made on the baby's forehead.

Most children in the village attended Sunday School and some came from a hamlet called Lower End in the next county. Of course we had to go to church as well, morning and evening, especially those of us who were in the choir. The choir took anyone who could warble a few bars.

On summer evenings after church whole families went for a walk. It was fun anticipating who else one would meet on the walk, perhaps a courting couple or someone from another village.

Miss Bennet the Sunday school teacher took all the children to Salford Wood on Good Fridays to gather primroses to put in the church for Easter. This yearly ritual was looked forward to.

For Mothering Sunday we gathered and put into bunches violets from under the hedgerows or picked snowdrops from Hulcote churchyard. We stood in the church porch to proudly present a bunch to each person arriving for the special Mothering Sunday service, the choice of flowers depending on whether Easter was early or late that year.

Our yearly Sunday school treat was to be invited up to Hulcote rectory for tea, games of croquet, paddling in the brook that ran at the bottom of the garden, or playing on the swing hanging from a large tree in the field in front of the rectory, kept I expect for us children. We all trudged home tired but happy, supervised by the faithful Miss Bennet.'

'The Sunday school Anniversary at Upper Dean between the wars was held every July. All the children dressed in their best and sang and recited. It was followed that week with a tea and games in the nearby farmer's field. Dads put up swings of cart ropes, slung over the oak tree branches, races were run and lots of fun was had by all.'

'The event of the year for us in Colesden was the annual Sunday school treat. Every resident helped in some way and we had delicious teas – but they could be a headache of organisation. My neighbour, one of the tea ladies, has told me many times that they did not know how many to cater for, as the then Colesden church room secretary would have invited many more children from surrounding villages. The ladies would have the task of fetching the water for the boiler from a standpipe 100 yards from the church room, which stood close by the entrance to Grange Farm driveway. After tea the room would be filled to capacity with the rest of Colesden's residents, when the Rev A.J.W. Pym gave out the Sunday school prizes, and the evening was filled with fun and games.'

'The Sunday school treat at Stanbridge in the 1940s was afternoon tea on the vicarage lawn, and an outing by coach starting at six in the morning and returning late evening, to Clacton or Southend.'

'Sunday school played a very big part in children's lives in Dunstable. Most would attend twice a day, and sometimes go to church or chapel as well. Outings are well remembered, to Harpenden Common, or Totternhoe Knolls, usually in a horse-drawn brake. It was a great occasion when the town churches combined for an outing by train to Southend.'

'When I was a child during the Second World War, most children in Harrold, the north Bedfordshire village in which I lived, went to Sunday school. My sisters and

I and most of our friends went to the Congregational chapel, as it was then called. We looked upon those children in the village who attended the parish church Sunday school as being very different – although I have no idea why.

Sunday was always the day for wearing our very best clothes. Sunday school was held in the afternoons from two to three. I suppose I was about three years old when I first attended. We were called the primary class. We learnt simple hymns and prayers and little rhymes and always had a Bible story. Then we did an activity – usually drawing a picture with crayons illustrating the story. We knelt on the floor, taking great care not to do the slightest bit of damage to our best clothes and used the seat of our chairs as makeshift desk tops.

When you reached the age of about seven you progressed into junior (or "big" as we called it) school. Much the same theme was used but we were split into groups for activities.

The highlights of the year were very different occasions. The Sunday school Anniversary was celebrated with great excitement on our part. For weeks before we had been taught special pieces of poetry and hymns and on the great day we marched into the "Big Church" which was full of parents and friends. We then performed our well rehearsed pieces with some of the less shy ones (including me) doing a solo. Oh how important we felt and how proud our parents were of us.

Another occasion which was anticipated with much excitement was the Sunday school outing. During the early years of the war this was only to a nearby farm. We had rides in a horse and cart, took it in turns on swings which had been put up in the orchard and then enjoyed a picnic tea. With the ending of the war we were able to do far more exciting things like going to Wickstead Park, Kettering. How hard it was to sleep the night before just thinking about the water chute, the train and all the other wonderful attractions at that park.

The Christmas party was cause for even more feverish excitement. After tea of sandwiches and cakes (rationing was still very much with us) we were entertained by a conjurer or film show – Mickey Mouse, Popeye and the like.

With the changing pattern of family life, with more working wives and mothers, Sunday has in many families become just another day. Indeed it is often one of the busiest days of the week around the home. Washing, ironing, car cleaning and now even shopping, as major supermarkets open, have changed beyond recognition those lovely family days we used to know.'

THE VICAR AND THE PARISH CLERK

'The rector of Roxton used to hold winter night school for teenagers in his library in the 1920s, no money needed. He was a brilliant scholar, an MA and former Master at Mill Hill. He wanted to see the young progress and he allowed me to borrow any books I required and encouraged my love of reading which I still enjoy in my eighties.'

'I was born in Potton and had a very happy childhood which can be summed up in this text which my mother often quoted to us: "Christ is the head of this household, an unseen guest at every meal and a silent listener at every conversation". There were two boys and two girls in the family.

My father worked in Miss Richardson's bakery shop in the Market Square. He was also the caretaker at the Conservative Club. In 1926 he was appointed Parish Clerk. The clerk was really the servant of the vicar. He dealt with baptisms, the calling of banns and the date of weddings. No-one, unless they were very important, was allowed to marry in Lent. The vicar would not have bridesmaids in church unless their heads were covered. The Rev Bagshaw was very strict. My father had a book of rules which he had to follow.

When anyone died he had to toll the bell. He got six pence for half an hour's work. It was the smallest bell for a child, and that was one stroke. For a woman it was the next bell and that was two strokes. For a man it was three strokes on the next bell. On the day of a funeral Dad and the vicar met the coffin at the church gate. In the early days it was a hand hearse. After the service Dad walked in front all the way to the cemetery. Men stopped and took off their hats when a funeral passed by.

Dad rang out the old year, and after the town clock had struck twelve he would ring in the new year. Sherry and mince pies were then served in the vicarage.

Dad was a very good ringer and could manage three bells at a time; one in his hand, one with his elbow and one with his foot. At harvest time we could sit in the vestry but we had to behave ourselves and not get off our seats. We thought our dad was the "Cat's

Whiskers" when he called the changes – "All Start Up",
"Two Trebles Gone". If the ringers got in a muddle he
would say "Rounds Next Time". It was an honour to ring
the bells.'

HOUSE & HOME

THE WAY WE LIVED THEN

The houses we lived in and the way of life we once took for granted have changed enormously over the past few decades. Houses were generally cold and draughty, with unheated bedrooms and cold linoleum on the floor. No wonder the warm kitchen, with a fire or range almost continuously alight for cooking and heating water, was a magnet for the whole family. Rag rugs were probably the nearest most families came to carpets and furniture was basic and made to last.

STONE AND THATCH

'In my early childhood I lived in an old stone and thatched cottage in Odell. Our house had a coal-fired range on which all the cooking was done, and the range was cleaned every day with black lead to keep it nice and shiny. In the hearth was a jam jar with a little paraffin in the bottom, in which we placed sticks to use as fire lighters. On the shelf was a cardboard box, full of spills made from folded-up newspaper, which were used for lighting the candles or oil lamp, and the old pipe.

The floor was very uneven, with flagstones. My mother used to make peg rugs, to lay on the floor for a covering. She would go to jumble sales and buy old coats, or any other thick materials of bright colour, to use for the rugs.

The inside walls of the house had several thicknesses of wallpaper. No plaster in those days – just wattle and daub. The bedrooms were very small, with low ceilings, and sometimes the windows were level with the floor and you had to get down on your knees to look out.

In the garden was a well, where we had to hook the bucket on to a long pole to get water for drinking, cooking and washing. We had an out-house with a copper in it, to get hot water, and a tin bath for bath night.

My father worked on the estate for the squire of the village. He was a keen gardener, and a regular church-goer. My mother had various jobs – working at the castle, caring for the sick by sitting up with them at night and as school caretaker for many years.

Mother and I used to go out in the fields collecting wood and sticks to help with the fuel. We also kept a few hens. After harvest we would go and pick up ears of corn, with the farmer's permission.

Last, but not least, was the toilet at the bottom of the garden. If one wanted to use it after dark, we had to light the lantern to find the way, and make plenty of noise to frighten away any rats which may have been about.'

A FAMILY OF TEN

'The family at Stevington consisted of eight children and two parents – there had been four infant deaths earlier from whooping cough and pneumonia. The children's ages were spread out, so four children were grown-up and away working. When the working children came home, the smaller ones had to sleep at their grandmother's home nearby.

The house had two large bedrooms, that consisted of

upstairs – no bathroom etc and of course no electric light, going to bed was by candlelight in each room.

There was a scullery, a living room – with black leaded stove for cooking, with an oven at the side.

Outside was a wash-house with brick copper; this was lit every Monday for wash days and Saturdays for baths, when the water was carried into the living room for the large tin bath – which all at home shared, being topped up from time to time. I remember my mother bathing us and washing our hair, and my father always rubbing our hair dry.

At the bottom of the garden was a bucket toilet in a small brick building.

The furnishings in the living room consisted of two armchairs and a sofa, a wooden table, covered by a chenille cloth with an oil lamp in the centre, plus eight wooden chairs (two of these were called Windsor and had arms).

The front garden, which was quite large, was always flowers. The back, also large, was vegetables and fruit trees, with a well for soft water for washing.

Drinking water was fetched in buckets from a well quite away from the house in the street. Dad had a yoke made to carry two buckets at one time, Mum only carried one bucket.

I remember wash days as always very hard work for my mother. She didn't own a mangle, but another neighbour did and used to charge a penny or twopence for use of same. At the end of the hard day, Mum always had a glass of "Porter".

Also in the garden were hen-houses and a pig sty, though later a law was passed to say that pigs were to be kept away from the house. The pigs and chickens were for food, and eggs, and we always had plenty of rabbits hanging on the back of the pantry door, caught by Dad.

I remember we never went hungry, we always had plenty of good food and were self sufficient. My father would purchase sides of cured pork from a neighbour who had kept his pigs away from the house and these were hung in the living room, and slices cut off when required. My mother always made her own jams and pickles from fruit and vegetables in the garden, and also made her own wine, ie dandelion etc.'

'Families were often large, most people were poor. Houses were sparsely furnished. The kitchen was the living room, with a blacklead range, using coal or wood collected from hedgerows and fallen trees. The kitchen was furnished with a plain whitewood scrubbed table, wooden chairs and a dresser for crockery. A cupboard usually built by the side of the fireplace contained cooking utensils.

Every Monday mums had to light the copper fire for boiling the washing. The copper was built in the corner of the scullery or in the outhouse. All cottons had to be boiled, linens and men's shirts. When dry all had to be ironed with heavy irons heated in front of the open fire. Mothers were very resourceful, never wasting anything, and making their own and children's clothes. A sewing machine was a treasured possession. Woollen jerseys and socks were hand-made. Fathers were great gardeners, providing vegetables and fruit all the year round, often taking on a strip of allotment to grow more. This caused the dads to have competitions at the annual village show, a very popular event, which is still held annually. Almost everyone went to church or chapel every Sunday. The chapel had a thriving Sunday school with a prize-giving day and a day out to the coast by charabanc.'

THE TIED COTTAGE

'Our house at Odell was a tied farm worker's stone cottage. We had one living room, one kitchen, two bedrooms, no bathroom and no running water. There was no sink or electricity and the toilet was in a shed at the bottom of the garden. Water was carried from a tap in the street, we had a black kitchen range for our fire and an oil lamp and candles for light.

Washing was done in a tin bath and put in a stone copper in the corner of the kitchen, a fire underneath burning rubbish and wood from the hedgerows. Then clothes were put through a mangle and hung outside to dry. Ironing was done with a flat iron heated on the fire.

We had a table, chairs, two high-backed chairs, a settee, a sideboard and a wireless, and lino and rugs on the floor. Bedrooms had brass and iron bedsteads, a dressing table, wardrobe and drawers, and a jug and basin to wash in and a chamber pot.

We grew most of the vegetables we needed, and we kept chickens. We had a well to get water for the garden.'

'In my early years I lived in a tied cottage at Colesden, a small hamlet in the parish of Roxton. Approximately 90 people lived there and nearly all worked on one of the four farms – Colesden Lodge and Grange farms owned by

W.L. Waddington, Bell Farm owned by the Bath family of Roxton Park Farm and finally New Farm, worked by the Wildman family. Each farm had tied cottages for their employees.

I recall in 1937 water mains being laid in Colesden, as in Roxton, where I first went to school in 1936, we had a standpipe outside the cottages to fetch water from.

For dark nights we had paraffin oil lamps. Our weekly grocer carried the paraffin in large cans on a rack fitted to his van. The shop was W.T. Lack & Sons of Channels End, Colmworth, and he also supplied us with candles which we used to see to go to bed.

Household tins and bottles were, like the contents of the outside closet pail, buried in a hole in the garden, where all our vegetables grew. In the evenings we had only a radio to listen to. Father mended our shoes and on dark evenings we spent hours tearing up pieces of material and cast off clothing to make rag rugs. Made by "pegging", most cottages had one in front of the fireplace and one outside the back door. This latter had two uses. Besides being a floor mat, one could use it to keep out the draughts in the winter time. The backing for these rugs was a hessian sack which had contained sugar beet pulp from the farm. To shake out the dust from a rag rug, it nearly pulled your arms out!'

AN ASPIDISTRA IN THE CORNER

'Houses were generally sparsely furnished and had lino or red tiles on the floor. Paintwork was universally brown. There was usually an outside toilet. The front room, or parlour, was used only on Sundays, or when there were visitors. An aspidistra normally stood in one corner (one of our members has one dating back at least 100 years), and the main piece of furniture was a large dresser. The fireplace was protected by a steel or brass fender and the surround usually black-leaded. In the kitchen was a bare wooden table, scrubbed clean, and a range on which all cooking would be done. A food safe would be housed in the cellar, if there was one.'

LEATHER ON THE FIRE

'Our house at Harrold was a brick built cottage in a row of eight. We had a room to sit in, a kitchen with a range for cooking, two bedrooms, no bathroom and no sink – water was pumped up from the well. Oil lamps and candles were used for light.

Washdays were very hard. All the water used had to be pumped from the well or taken from a barrel containing rainwater. A stone copper was used to boil the clothes. Pieces of leather from the local factory were used on the fire under the boiler.

We had chairs, a table, a couchbox with toys in, a wireless and a gramophone, a washstand, iron bedsteads, chests of drawers and wardrobes. On the floor we had lino with rugs. Vegetables and fruit were grown and we kept chickens and a pig.'

SWEEPING THE CHIMNEY

'My father swept the large chimney of our cottage at Stanbridge by pulling a faggot of sticks through to remove the soot.'

RUGS AND RAGS

'The floor was covered with sacks that the corn was put into or rugs made from old clothes. Rugs for the bedroom were made out of coloured dresses and undergarments. They were cut into strips and plaited together, shaped in a circle and stitched together. Cushions were made of patchwork and there were lace mats for the table.'

'Furniture was sparse with a "scrubbed" table, chairs for meals and an armchair for father, sometimes a sofa. Before the fire would be a hearth rug. These were made from a large piece of sackcloth, patiently pegged with a special hook on a handle. Material cut about six inches by one inch was drawn through the sacking, staying firmly in place. Not much pattern could be worked as mostly oddments were used, but a good warm rug materialised for comfort last thing at night when the family sat round the fire. A chenille tablecloth covered the scrubbed table for cosiness. One drawback of the heavy fireside rug was the taking outside to shake out the dirt. Some homes had a parlour with a better rug, an easy chair and a few ornaments and pictures. This was often kept for special occasions, often a very hallowed room indeed.'

END OF TERRACE

'Gilded by nostalgia into a veritable palace, my 1940s home was in fact a modest end-of-terrace house which belonged to my father's employers. We were fortunate in those war years to be a complete family, due to my father's reserve occupation.

I remember how the front door opened straight onto the street. This door led into a narrow hall with that holy-of-holies, the parlour, on the left. This unwelcoming room, with its rigid furniture and formal tidiness, was kept locked. Only on Sunday afternoons and for my daily piano practice would the stiff key be turned and the cold still air be ruffled. At the end of the hall, our living room was also to the left. This room was where we ate, played, rested and spent the majority of our time together. The room was dominated by a large range, with a china-loaded dresser at each side. It was my task to black-lead this range every Saturday, to Cardinal polish the red tiled hearth, and, worst of all to Brasso the fender which read "Home Sweet Home". Much as I hated these tasks they were infinitely preferable to those of my brother. He had to take out the bucket and shovel after the milk-cart had been! Dad, you see, grew vegetables. All our cooking was done on this range, until "The Gas" was laid on in the scullery. The fire was kept alight, and in winter our clothes would be warmed in the huge oven.

Upstairs the three bedrooms were like ice-boxes, for, unless one was ill in bed, fires were not lit in their grates. In the cold months a wary face poked from beneath the bedding would see that Jack Frost had decorated the window panes and stiffened the curtains so that they crackled when touched. At Mother's third, or even fourth call, out would pop my testing leg. Then with a frantic leap I'd jump onto the clippy rug beside my bed, hop onto the lino and rush downstairs to the brightness of our living room. A cheerful hug and kiss from Mother, who would then admonish me to "Be quick" and I would be out of my nightie, quickly washed in a bowl and into

my warm clothes before you could say "Lampton Worm".
Breakfast was usually bread and milk (which I adored)
followed by a tablespoon of cod liver oil and malt. Then
I felt ready to face whatever the day would bring.

Happy days, short on wealth and luxuries, but long
on love and hope. Thank you God for my childhood
home.'

THE FAMILY ROUTINE

The memory of washday still strikes cold in the hearts
of those who experienced its sheer drudgery week after
week. From the lighting of the copper to the mangling,
the drying and the ironing, it meant hours of hard work
for the housewife. Water, of course, had to be fetched,
drop by drop, from the rain butt, well or standpipe,
as it did when bathnight came round too. There was
no question of a flush toilet, for most families it was
a bucket privy down the garden – not pleasant on a
dark night! This did, however, have its benefits for the
vegetable garden or allotment.

THROUGH THE WEEK

'Most village homes at Salford and Hulcote were of the
two or three bedroom type, with often one bedroom being

an open landing. All had good sized gardens given over primarily to fruit and vegetable growing.

The water came from an outside well or pump, there being no mains water in the village until the later years of the 1930s. Farm houses had their own well or pump but cottages had one between two, three or even four houses depending whether they were detached, semi, or terraced dwellings.

Nearly every home had a barrel for catching rain water, to be used for washing clothes, hair and bodies. Pump or well water was sweet to drink but took a lot of soap if it had to be used for washing clothes.

Bath night was usually Friday, in the tin bath in front of the fire in winter and in the outside washhouse in summer. Youngest first going up in order of age, a little more hot water from the copper being added for each person.

Cooking was done on kitchen ranges using coal and wood. Flues had to be cleaned out once a week or the oven would not get hot. The range was blackleaded daily and the steel fenders rubbed with emery paper. In hot weather paraffin cookers were often used instead. No one had electricity until the mid 1930s and then only a few, the remainder relying on paraffin lamps and candles.

Floor covering tended to be linoleum and pegged rugs. Very few had carpets. The kitchen, a gathering place for the family, had a scrubbed wooden table and upright chairs. Front rooms (as we called them) were for Sunday and holiday use, the furniture a sofa and a few upholstered chairs and maybe a polished table. Front doors were hardly ever opened.

All cleaning was done manually, floors scrubbed and polished on hands and knees, lamp glasses washed and lamp wicks trimmed once a week. The annual spring cleaning was an event. Carpets were taken out and beaten on the line, blankets washed and larders where the food was kept whitewashed. The larders were filled with jam, pickles and preserves made in season with produce from the garden.'

'Our memories of days gone by in Great Barford are many and varied. The women worked extremely hard in the home – how easy life is today with all modern appliances. There was no electricity, only oil lamps which had to be cleaned and filled, the wicks trimmed each day before dark. Candles and night-lights to go to bed with, many children making shadow figures with their hands before falling asleep. Bathrooms did not exist, "aunties" at the bottom of the garden were the only form of lavatory and chamber pots for bedroom use. Bath night was usually Friday and the ritual of bathing in front of the kitchen fire in a large zinc bath was known to all.

As there was no running water system, rain water was

collected in large water butts and drinking water fetched from the village wells each day. Rain water was used for bathing and clothes washing and "washday" was usually Mondays which many children knew as "soapsuds and Bubble and Squeak" day, meaning the house seemed to be filled with the smell of washing and the cold vegetables from Sunday lunch were mashed together and fried to be served with cold meat. The ritual of Mondays was the filling of the copper with water and lighting and stoking the fire underneath to bring the water to boiling point, the "best whites" taking the first wash. Recketts Blue bags were added to the final rinse to keep the whites as white as possible. The clothes were then put through the mangle to extract as much water as possible, before being taken out to the washing lines, which were made of rope and possibly hung between fruit trees. You always hoped for a gentle wind to help dry the washing but not enough to break the rope, so causing the washing to trail across the garden and become soiled again.

Ironing day was usually Tuesdays, the irons being heated in front of the kitchen fire. When you thought they were hot enough you always gave them a quick rub on the hearthrug to ensure they were clean. Clothes were then placed on a wooden clothes-horse to air, in summer out of doors, in winter around the kitchen-fire.

The houses were very cold in winter with draughts from both windows and doors. The kitchen was the most used room because the fire was always alight as this was the means of cooking, though some homes had paraffin stoves for use in the very hot weather. Floors were usually of stone or quarry tiles and coconut matting and rag rugs were used to cover them. Wooden floors were either polished or covered with linoleum and occasional rugs, with sheepskin rugs by the side of the bed if you were lucky.

Thick curtains were hung at windows and doors, always lined and sometimes interlined with old blankets. These were taken down at spring-cleaning time and replaced with light curtains of cretonne or chintz. Beds had both flock mattresses and feather beds, icy cold linen sheets and heavy woollen blankets, as well as eiderdowns and quilts and bedcovers, what a weight they were!

The kitchen table acted as many things; food preparation area, ironing board, desk or children's play area. It was usually covered with a chenille cloth which reached the ground, and table cloths of either gingham or damask depending on which meal was taken. Sunday tea was special with a lace cloth on top of the damask one and at least two kinds of cake as well as scones and sandwiches.

Life may have been hard work for our mothers but very fond memories remain of a winter's Sunday afternoon tea with the fire ablaze and the table looking a picture with the best cloth and china.'

'I remember our house being light and airy but also draughty and damp, clothes needed airing before being worn. Most of our furniture was a mixture in size and style, having moved from a small to a larger farmhouse. Some of the new furniture was heavy and fairly ornate with plenty of dust traps. Carpets were surrounded by polished floors which needed dusting every day, cleaning tools available were carpet sweeper or dustpan and brush, creating lots of dust. I used to enjoy that because I could really see where I had been with the duster. Lighting was by oil lamps or candle which often smoked. Baths were taken in the zinc bath and the lavatory was outside, we had three varied in height just like the three bears.

Washdays really were wash *days*; the laundry was soaked overnight in the zinc bath and/or boiled in the large brick copper. It was then rinsed in blue-bag water, and put through a massive wooden mangle before being hung outside. My mother used to break off to cook the dinner and continue after washing up. Ironing meant flat irons heated against the front bars of the kitchen range. The garden was not as well tended as today, a mown lawn with a few perennials . . . flowers which had to stand up to free range hens and geese before the garden was enclosed.'

'Homes in the 1920s had few amenities – no domestic appliances beyond the copper in the kitchen under which a fire had to be lit before boiling the clothes. No vacuum cleaners, only carpet sweepers. And only a carpet square in the best room. No electricity, but gaslight and flat irons heated over the gas. No radio, no fridges – a cold slab in the larder with mesh covers to keep off the flies. Food was bought daily in hot weather. Flies were commonplace in the home – lots of them. Before flypapers were introduced one could buy round containers in the bottom of which beer was poured which attracted the flies. When the container was buzzing with flies it was plunged into a bucket of water to drown the flies! When electricity first came in it was possible to have one room converted at a time – advertised at the time as "£1 a point".'

'Women's work was never done – cooking, cleaning, mending and jam making and if they could they made pillow lace to buy clothes for the children.'

WASHDAY

'Washday was a major operation in my young days. We lived in an old farmhouse and the kitchen had at one time been the brewhouse. It contained a huge copper in one corner, but this was seldom used as it held so much water, and an open hearth on which huge logs were burned, at times balanced on bricks because of the length and pushed up as they burned. The floor sloped to the centre and to clean it, it was swilled with the washing water and brushed with a hard brush, the water running out through a small hole in the outside wall. Water was carried by the bucketful from down the cowyard, there was no mains water in the house. Large baths and spare buckets were filled with water, which was heated in an iron pot resting on two flat iron bars over the hearth.

Before washing commenced, the chairs were carried out into the passage which connected the kitchen to the main part of the house, and the table was pushed to one wall to allow plenty of space in the centre. The washing was sorted into piles – whites, colours, then socks and trousers. In this order they were all washed in the same water, then followed another wash for the dirtiest clothes. Two rinses were required, after which things were put through a mangle, taking care to fold the buttons to the inside to avoid breakages. Items to be boiled were put into another iron pot on the hearth, pushing them down with a copperstick. If you were lucky no soot fell down into the white washing, if not, and it could not be carefully lifted out – more washing! At spring cleaning time there were curtains, blankets and bedspreads to be washed by hand.

If everything went smoothly we would be cleared up and the kitchen back to normal by dinnertime, in the middle of the day then; if not we had to stop, get the men's dinner and finish afterwards, which made an extra long washday. Hopefully by this time some of the thinner items were dry enough to iron. The old fashioned flat irons were heated in front of the fire, one getting hot whilst another was in use. Great care had to be taken to clean the iron each time or you would be sure to get a black mark on the clothes, always where it showed, of course, which meant more washing. The sheets and towels were folded when dry and again put through the mangle. This saved a lot of ironing but was still hard work turning the handle at the end of a long and tiring day. If it was wet weather the washing still went ahead but the wet washing hung about the house for several days. Washday tempers were rather thin and sometimes frayed.'

'Washday in the early 1920s was, in my opinion, the worst day of the week. We all put our clothes out for washing and Mother would do the sorting out – the articles for boiling and ordinary washing. The ones for boiling would be put in a large brick (lined with copper) contraption filled with water, underneath which was a fire – this had to be lit and got going a while before the clothes were added with soap or whatever one used. When the boiling had finished, the rinsing had to be

80

done in several changes of water. The wash was then put through the mangle. The mangle was huge, with big wooden rollers, and it took quite a lot of strength to turn the handle and get all the water removed. The rest of the washing was done by hand and mangled in the same manner. All this took up most of the morning and drying outside all the afternoon. That is why we always had Bubble and Squeak and cold meat for dinner that day.'

'I was born in the 1920s in a two-up, two-down rented house, end of terrace of four, at Wootton. Washday took my mother nearly all day. She washed in a brick built barn with a copper one end and coal the other. All water was drawn in buckets from a pump in the middle of the four gardens. The whites were washed first, then put in the copper to boil. The copper was urged on with cardboard, wood and slack coal (the coal dust and small pieces). After a good boil, the whites were removed from the copper, rinsed twice (and tablecloths etc starched) and put through a large wooden-rollered mangle before hanging it out to dry on a line all down the back garden.'

'Monday was washday and this was done in a copper

that was built in the corner of the scullery. We had to collect wood to burn underneath it to boil the water. To the water was added soda and grated white soap. We used zinc baths to wash and rinse the clothes in. A bowl of starch was used for tablecloths, pinafores and shirt collars – shirts did not have collars attached. The pegs for hanging out were hand-made from sycamore wood, which was collected from the woods and hedgerows. After the washing was finished, the scullery floor had to be scrubbed as there were no carpets on the floor. If the men were ill and no money came in, then the women would take in extra washing to earn a few shillings to feed their family.'

OUT TO THE PRIVY

'The privy at my mother's house at Kempston in the early 1900s was reached across a cobbled yard and was a bench with three holes, a large one, a middle one and a small one with a step in front. About 1908 the pit was filled in and buckets installed. These were emptied once a week about five o'clock in the morning.'

'Life in rural Bedfordshire was truly spartan at the beginning of this century as commodities that we take for granted were lacking. Few homes had tapped water so a well in the garden had to suffice for this necessity of life, often drawn up with a long pole with a hook on the end to hold the bucket. Ponds in the village watered the animals, yet these dried up in hot summers, making work – a tank on wheels had to be pulled by a horse several miles to the river.

The toilet was set well away from the house, perhaps at the end of the garden, to avoid the smell, especially those with just a bucket set under a wooden seat with a hole cut round. These were regularly emptied into a hole in the garden. Others known as earth closets had a large hole with a seat and access to the back. Each time this was used a sprinkling of ashes was shaken in with a small shovel. It was cleared annually with a shovel and truck.'

'At Bletsoe between the two world wars the rows of brick built terraced houses opened straight onto the road. There was only a small yard behind and that had the bucket lavatory in it. However, there were allotments and the villagers emptied the buckets onto this open land. No wonder the vegetables subsequently grown there were so fine.'

'Stevington was one of the first villages to be on the mains sewer, but only if you were lucky enough to live on the right side of the road in Silver Street. This was well before the war in 1939. The sewer beds had to be kept clear and this was done by Percy Keech very early in the morning – as he returned home he could be heard singing so beautifully.'

BATH AND A CANDLE TO BED

'On bathnight in the 1920s a long, galvanised bath was brought in and put before the kitchen range. The water was heated in saucepans and in a large black kettle. My younger sister sat at one end and I sat at the other end.'

'I remember seeing the huge copper jugs in Tempsford rectory kitchen that were taken upstairs in the early morning to the huge hip bath in a room exclusive to bathing. Most families had a weekly bath in the back kitchen, in cold weather in front of the fire.'

'One of my first memories is of going upstairs to bed with a candlestick, a special one made of green pottery, with a shield at the back so that the candle did not go out. I was not allowed to light the gas in my bedroom, and in any case it was too high up for me to reach.

At Sunday school we sang a hymn "Jesus bids us shine with a pure clear light, like a little candle burning in the night". The next verse had a line "Well he sees and knows us, though our light grows dim". Like most children, I learned the words by rote and it was not until some years later when I could read well, that I realised that I had always sung (quite logically) "Jesus bids us shine with a poor queer light" and "Well he sees our noses". Each verse finishes with "You in your small corner and I in mine" and I used to imagine myself sitting on a stool in the corner of my bedroom with my candlestick and the light – the poor queer light, shining on my nose.'

ON THE ALLOTMENT

'Gardening was a great pastime at Stevington but priority was given to anything that could be eaten. Many men had allotments. Corn was grown as well as the vegetables and in the early years of the century it was ground into flour at the windmill in the village. We never bought vegetables or flour. Later, when the windmill fell into disrepair, the wheat was ground at Quenby's mill in Bromham.

The threshing machine was hired at Stevington Feast for the whole village to thresh their wheat – in the middle of September my father would take his only holiday of three days to help with the threshing. If he noticed a particular field had an excellent yield of wheat, we children were sent to glean and the seed was kept for the next year.'

'Gardens, although they had a few flowers, were for growing food – all kinds of vegetables, particularly swedes, parsnips, carrots, onions and others that could be stored for winter. All villages seemed to have allotments. The men worked at least until one o'clock on Saturdays, but many villagers met on the allotments on Saturday afternoons. Wives and children went too, admired each other's produce and gathered Sunday requirements. Very rarely early in this century would men be seen on the allotments on Sunday, though the Second World War and the pressing circumstances of the time seemed to bring a change from "No work on Sundays".'

'The cottage gardens at Roxton at the beginning of the century were cultivated to grow fruit and vegetables for the winter, and most men also had a rood of ground for growing wheat that was thrashed by flail on a farm barn floor. Later it was ground by millers for making family loaves to feed the large families, often comprising of up to ten children.'

TRADERS TO THE DOOR

There was a time, not so long ago, when you hardly needed to stir from your front door to go shopping. Everything from bread to wet fish, cotton reels to fancy garters, could be purchased from one of the many traders who toured the villages of Bedfordshire week by week.

ALMOST EVERYTHING WE NEEDED

'When I was young, in Wymington in the 1920s, almost everything we needed could be brought to our doors by horse-drawn drays, carts, floats, traps, tradesmen's bikes and men on foot.

We had three greengrocers call regularly, carrying seasonal fruit and vegetables (oranges from Christmas to March, and no salad stuff in winter).

In our small town, all 16 butchers delivered on six days a week if required; their boys pedalled round the heavy bikes with baskets piled high with paper-wrapped orders. I can recall ten bakers, all with delivery carts. Ours was the "Midnight Baker" whose late hours led him to leave loaves in somewhat unhygienic places, but his bread was delicious. Our milkman lugged round his four-gallon can with the pint and half-pint dippers hanging inside, while his horse and float kept pace with him. Most of the grocers delivered whenever customers wished, though the Co-op cart came round only on Fridays, as did the fishmonger with herrings, bloaters and smoked haddock kept fresh on a block of ice. A confectioner with a pony trap called on Saturday afternoons, when I spent my halfpenny, which bought a bar of toffee, or ten aniseed balls or a sherbet fountain. The other man came on Wednesdays, selling cakes and biscuits as well as sweets. Two haberdashers had regular rounds, one walking with a basketful of mending wools, a penny a skein, needles and cottons, tapes, buttons and elastic. The other pedalled an enormous hamper on wheels and he brought much more stock – socks, stockings, underwear, pinafores and aprons.

A man came every week with a special margarine and tins of dried milk with Virol for hot drinks. Another came with packets of cake and sponge pudding mixes, and a young handicapped man called monthly with note-paper and envelopes.

Regularly, but less often came the coalman, whose heavy dray carried huge scales to weigh the enormous lumps of shiny coal which he then "barrowed" to our barns. Lumps could weigh over a cwt.

Then there were men on the road with cases packed with fancy goods – silk scarves, fancy garters, scented soap, combs, mirrors, and "diamond" hairslides for three-pence. Some had patent medicines, Sno-fire for chapped hands, camphorated oil for wheezy chests, pills for all ills. Gipsies sold brushes, lace by the yard, paper flowers and clothes pegs, all costing only a few pence. One old woman offered packets of dried lavender so old it had no scent. People rarely took one, they were so grubby, but just gave her the penny, but she was not begging – an offence in those days.

These, together with the rent-man, post-man, paper-boys and the doctor were our regular callers. There was an ice-cream man with a donkey cart, later on also a Walls ice cream man with his "Stop Me And Buy One" slogan and the barrel-organ man. All these, and many more. I haven't even mentioned the tramps!'

'Market days in the 1930s were Bletchley Thursday and Bedford Saturday. Practically everything could be purchased, from livestock to clothes finery and household goods. However, nearly everything a person could want was brought to the door, making a trip to to the town from Salford for marketing or shopping something of an outing.

Bread was delivered to the door by three different bakers each having their special days, though some did coincide. Once a week a pastry cook came round with cream cakes.

A man came to take the grocery order at the beginning of the week and the goods were delivered later in the week. The goods were paid for when the next order was taken. Some grocers only came fortnightly though.

Milk was brought to the door daily by a local farmer and decanted from a large vessel via a pint measure into the waiting jug. A few households fetched their own milk in aluminium cans straight from the farm. Skimmed milk could be purchased for a penny a pint from a trader who made butter.

Travelling salesmen of all kinds came round selling a variety of wares. One was called the "Wednesday Man" and sold general hardware. A wet fish van called every Friday, summoning customers by ringing his bell. A Mr Nightingale used to come with a large suitcase strapped on the back of his bicycle containing odds and ends suitable for sewing and small household repairs, and of course gipsies called from time to time with clothes pegs and fortune telling. On Thursday evenings a fried fish van paid its weekly visit. A bag of chips cost a penny. In the summer a Walls ice-cream cart was pedalled round and two other vendors came selling home-made ice-cream.

When the village post office changed premises in the mid 1930s, the new postmistress sold all sorts of commodities beside postal requirements. The Swan pub also had a room at the back for selling a few general groceries and sweets. Until the latter part of the decade a little shop on the edge of the village sold sweets, bootlaces, blacklead, washing aids and small household requirements. This shop was presided over by a little old lady in a blue and white check apron. Here we spent our Saturday pennies. Letters and parcels were delivered twice daily by a postman on a bicycle.'

THE BAKER, THE MILKMAN . . .

'Shopping in the early 1920s was much easier than now. There was always a corner shop near by, which sold everything you could think of and need, and also there were the horse and cart traders, who came round the streets most days. For instance, the greengrocer had a huge cart packed with every vegetable and fruit available at that time of year. The produce was home grown and fresh so there were no worries about that. He also provided paraffin oil if needed! A baker called three or four times a week with freshly baked bread and cakes. A fishmonger and a butcher would send a boy round on a bicycle to take your order and deliver it in about half an hour so that you could cook it that same day. Milk was delivered on a cart in a big milk churn and was ladled out into your own jug at the doorstep. On Saturdays the muffin man used to ring a bell and we would go out and buy whatever we wanted and eat them hot and crisp with lots of butter and celery. People were so pleasant in those days and happy to serve you.'

'In the 1920s at Wootton the milk, delivered by horse and cart, was taken from large churns in measuring cans, then poured into the milk jugs at the householder's door. In the summer milk had to be boiled – no fridges then, and how we hated the skin that formed on the top. The baker delivered freshly baked bread, also by horse and cart; fresh hot cross buns were delivered early on Good Friday mornings. The village butcher cycled around the village to sell his meat.'

'We had five family grocer's shops in the small village of Langford Ivel and we always did our shopping locally. My mother used to write an order and they delivered it. A van would come round with paraffin and all hardware items, our bread was always delivered, and a greengrocer called every week.'

'In the 1940s I can remember the milk being brought round Sharnbrook by horse and cart and my mother taking a jug out for Jean to measure out each pint. One of my earliest memories is playing at being a "milk lady" – my grandfather made me a measure which hooked over a bucket and that kept me happy for hours.'

LONG JOHN AND MISS LIGHTFOOT

'Many traders, known as packmen, used to come into Stevington. Long John came once a week from Bedford on his bicycle, carrying a large bundle containing such things as shirts, underpants and tea towels. Miss Lightfoot came in a taxi and sold practically everything – sheets, clothes, shoes. You could send her a letter asking for something special and she would bring it on her next visit. She was very smart and very heavily made up, and she always wore a hat.

Browning & Sons came with groceries and lovely biscuits; also Dudeney & Johnstons, Grimbley Hughes and a Mr Sargent who came on a bicycle. Such things as paraffin and carbolic soap were provided by Sowman of Olney, who came once a month. Friday nights were fish and chip nights – twopence for a big parcel. A men's tailor used to call three times a year.

The chimney sweep who came from Felmersham was a real character. He would sweep one chimney, then have some home-made wine, do another chimney, have some more wine, then sit on the Cross and sing like billy-o. The housewives all used to be round him trying to persuade him to go to their house next as they could not cook the meal until their chimney was swept.

Every autumn the Blackberry Man came. Coming from Rushden, he stood at the Cross ringing his bell to announce his arrival. He came to collect berries used for dye. Every hedge would be a scene of activity as children rushed to fill baskets after school to gain a bit of pocket money.

Several people delivered milk in cans – George Wooding on his bike, Charlie Warwick, Aunt Berth (who wore a tweed cap and came with a yoke, plus a large sackful of hay on her shoulder), Harry Middleton, and then Fred Horner from Bromham, who was such a cheerful man and was always whistling and could be heard long before he arrived.'

THE HOKEY POKEY MAN

'In summer days in Lidlington in the 1920s we waited for the Hokey Pokey Man. He came from Cranfield in an open-topped car with ice-filled, double-walled containers of his home-made ice cream on the back seats. He rang a handbell and we children ran from all directions. I used to buy two penny cornets. One was for my dog Jock, an Airedale Terrier I grew up with, who loved it as much as I did. My parents made ice cream once. Father had to collect the ice from Bedford, wrapped in sacks, in his motorbike and sidecar. Sadly for me, it was only once, as it was very hard work and messy.'

FOOD, DRINK AND THE CLOTHES WE WORE

In today's world of ready-meals for the microwave it is difficult to imagine the work that went into making food to feed the family. Preparing meat, especially after the pig-killing, baking bread and pies for the week, pickling and preserving for the winter ahead was all a time consuming business. Clothing too was simpler then – no fashion shops for children and teenagers – it was a case of handed down and handed on for most. Stylish dress took very much second place to clothes that kept you warm and dry.

GRANDMA'S ELDERBERRY WINE

'My father, a North Bedfordshire man, related the following tale to us as children in the 1920s.

Grandmother, an industrious woman who could turn her hand to any domestic chore, had been making elderberry wine and had disposed of the fermented berries down the bottom of the orchard. On going to her chickens, she was surprised to see them all lying around dead. Resigned to going without eggs, but determined to have roast chicken, she set to work, plucked them all and placed them on the kitchen table overnight. The following day she was met by the sight of her chickens all running around completely naked, and feeling sorry for them promptly made them each a red flannel vest to wear until their feathers grew again.

As we grew older we wondered about the authenticity of this tale but an elderly cousin later verified this story as true!'

PIGS AND GLEANING

'Nearly all cottagers at Roxton kept two pigs in a sty outside the back door, one went to market and one was killed for home consumption. The best joints were salted in a pork pot and the back hams were used for special occasions such as weddings, funerals and christenings. Home-made wine was made by many from garden fruit, with blackberries, sloes and elderberries free from the hedgerows. Women and children all went gleaning corn, barley and oats – the corn for bread flour, the barley and oats for the pigs. A gleaning bell was rung in harvest time from Roxton church tower at eight in the morning and again at six in the evening, so as to ensure fair shares for all gleaners. Village boundaries were vigorously kept, any stray ladies were sent back to their own parish with dire warnings not to come again.'

KEEPING WARM

'Days before central heating were no fun. My father got up first and would light the boiler which heated the water. This was fine as long as the wind was not in the east – then the fire just would not go! The boiler heated the kitchen so this was snug, but the only other heat was a coal fire in the living room. On a winter's morning it took a great deal of willpower to get out of bed, especially when there was thick ice on the inside of the windows!

We were always encouraged to wash our hair in soft water that we would get out of the water butt and boil in a saucepan on the electric stove. And we were never allowed to step outside until at least half an hour had elapsed after taking a bath! And, of course, the answer to every ill, the highly revered article of clothing, the vest (never to be left off under any circumstances). My mother and I had endless arguments about the wearing of one and I once cut mine off at the waist and blanket stitched round them so that they wouldn't ruckle up. Needless to say mother was furious with me! The liberty bodice was discarded in the summer months – oh joy!'

WASP WAISTS

'Corsets and stays were very much the fashion early in the century to give women the wasp waists and curves desirable at the time. After childbirth, it was common practice for some women to use "binders" to bind up the abdomen, some going so far as to place a book over the abdomen to flatten it still further before binding up.'

HATS FOR ALL SEASONS

'"Where did you get that hat, where did you get that tile?
    Isn't it a nobby one, in quite the latest style."

My father would sing this old music hall song whenever we appeared in a new home-made creation, just as he regaled us with "Tell me the old, old story" if we tried to make lame excuses.
    But back to hats. Everyone wore hats, from the men with their bowlers and caps and trilbys to Queen Mary with her eternal toques. Our hats were often home-made. A cheap stiff buckram shape from the milliner was covered with soft material and trimmed with bows, flowers or ribbon pompoms. A new hat needed to match a new coat? The old cover was removed and the buckram

recovered and voilà – a new hat! I remember a hat of my mother's, dark velvet trimmed with giant velvet pansies all round the crown.

In winter, bobble hats were close fitting and snug over the ears, with a huge bobble of wool on top, or two smaller bobbles on strings fixed to one side like overgrown cherries. A neighbour ran a small milliner's business in her front room. She would go up to Luton on the train to buy her stock. Most was untrimmed and she would add the finishing touches to her customers' requirements. It was a great event to have a "boughten" hat, tried on in Mrs B's front room and regarded in her large mirror, using a small hand mirror to get a side or back view. From her, as we grew older, we bought our school velours and panamas, which were trimmed with house bands and badges bought elsewhere. At first Mother insisted on a bonnet shape, with an unrolled brim that was slightly wider at the sides than back or front. Later we were allowed to have the traditional school hat with equal width brim, worn up at the back and down at the front. That was how it should be worn, but being girls full of individuality we found other ways – up all round, like a Breton sailor, or down all round a la Garbo, or up on one side like an Australian soldier. There was no end to our ingenuity with the simple school hat with its elastic under the chin.

The dry cleaners of those days offered a cleaning and re-blocking service for a small charge. The felt or panama was steamed to the requisite floppiness and pressed over the selected head block. Add a pretty trim and it was as good as new. I remember one lovely thick black shiny velour that I inherited from my maternal grandma, and after reblocking I wore it with great panache!

The war came, and with resources needed for the Services, hats were less worn. Instead long scarves were tied turban-wise to keep our heads covered, or triangular scarves were tied under the chin, peasant style, or we wore cheeky berets. Sadly, the high days of the hat were gone for ever.'

FROM THE CRADLE TO
THE GRAVE

Weddings were not lavish affairs for most Bedfordshire couples, and a honeymoon away from the village was an unattainable dream for those who had to put work first. Home births were the rule rather than the exception, helped either by the midwife or a local woman who would probably also list her duties as laying out the dead. Before the NHS, doctors had to be paid for and were not therefore to be consulted for minor illnesses – home remedies were relied on instead, some of which sound worse than the ailments they were meant to cure! An illustration of how far back living memory can reach is contained in the story of the brave little girl of the 1860s who, after having her finger amputated without anaesthetic, had to walk five miles home because there was no transport back to her village.

COURTING AND MARRIAGE

'Doris met her husband on what would now be called a "blind date" but which turned out not to be so, as Doris relates. Her friend Florrie had her eye on a young man who would only go out with her provided that a certain Jack Powers came along too, so Doris was asked to make up the four. On having Jack pointed out to her, Doris declined saying "I couldn't possibly – his nose is too big!" But at a later date Jack Powers, encountering the two girls together, introduced himself and said to Doris "I believe we are going out together" and to Florrie's astonishment she heard Doris say "Yes". Such was Jack Powers' charm that very soon after the first walking out, Doris found herself proposed to and accepting, and they were married when Doris was 18½ and Jack about 27. Doris and Jack soon realised that they had met years before when Doris was very small and Jack came to her home as a friend of her brothers. Jack did not remember Doris at the time!

They set up home in Naseby Road, Luton in a house bought for them by Jack Powers' father and had four children, two boys and two girls. At this point it's an interesting fact that Doris remembers becoming acquainted with birth control – the Dutch cap and pessaries being available as far back as 1926 or thereabouts.'

'At Stevington in the 1920s weddings were not expensive affairs. There was no tiered wedding cake, just an ordinary fruit cake iced, and the reception would take place at the home. The bride had a new dress but the guests, mainly family, would not buy new clothes, though some might have a new hat.'

BIRTHS AND CHRISTENINGS

'My youngest brother was born at home in Bromham in the 1940s. I can remember waking to my mother's cries of pain and feeling terrified. He was a premature breech baby and I learned later that he and my mother were lucky to be alive. At the age of nine I had to cope with the running of the house and family. No help was available to us and my father feared for his job at the London Brick Company and dared not have time off.'

'When my mother went into labour at our home in Sharnbrook in the 1930s, a towel was tied across the top of the bed for her to grip during contractions. When the baby was born the towel was threadbare. Give me the gas and air any day! When my husband was born, his father walked from Knotting to Sharnbrook to fetch the midwife, upwards of three miles. She had only just learned to ride a bike and she kept falling off all the way back to Knotting. It must have been a very fraught journey.'

'Christenings at Stevington were always held on the first Sunday in the month at the local church and probably three or four other babies were being christened at the same time.'

'Christenings at Stanbridge were held after Sunday school in the afternoon.'

TWO BRAVE LITTLE GIRLS

'Little Lucy Burnham was sent to spend days at a time to play with a little girl of about three years old who lived at Warden Hill Farm, which was located about five miles from the centre of Luton and at that time, around the 1860s, deep in the Bedfordshire countryside. On the day in question the little girls were chasing each other around a crushing machine, used for crushing wheat in those days, with a handle at the side. As Lucy ran round the machine she put her hand on the edge of the crusher at the same time as her little friend caught her apron in the handle of the machine, bringing it down and crushing Lucy's hand. When the handle released the crusher and Lucy's hand, she had the presence of mind to pick up an old tin lying around. dipping it into a horse trough in the farmyard and washing the blood off her hand, whilst the other little girl ran screaming to the farmhands for help.

The farmer and her mother had gone out for the day in their horse and trap so the farmhands, after wrapping the child's hand up, did not know what to do next, there being no transport on the farm available to take the child to a doctor. However, fate took a hand and a carter with a horse and cart came into the farmyard delivering supplies to the farm. The carter offered immediately to take the child into Luton to a doctor but said that he could not undertake to make the return journey back. However, this difficulty was not considered at the time, the urgency was to get the child to a doctor. So off went the farmhand and Lucy Burnham on the carter's cart to a doctor then resident in Mill Street.

The doctor sat Lucy on his knee and dealt with her

crushed hand – the first finger on the right hand lost part of the bone but otherwise was saved but the middle finger had to be amputated to the second joint and was twice as fat as originally. The doctor without anaesthetic for the child, dealt with the injury and bound the hand up and put the arm in a sling, saying to the farmhand: "I want to give this child something to make her sleep – can you take her somewhere where she can lie down for a few hours?", to sleep off presumably the shock of the accident. This the farmhand did, taking her to some people who lived in a row of small cottages just inside the Old Bedford Road.

The farmhand, to pass the time while Lucy slept, and no doubt in need of a restorative drink, repaired to the small pub nearby (The Rabbit) where he stayed as long as he could while Lucy slept off the nasty experience. Later in the day feeling rather "cheerful" after a pint or so of the local beer, he went back to the cottage and woke up little Lucy saying "Wake up Lucy, we've got to get you home". Bearing in mind that there was no public transport in the 1860s, horses and traps being the main means of transport apart from walking, the farmhand and little Lucy had no alternative but to walk the five miles or so to Warden Hill Farm. The farmhand, still feeling quite "happy" and to distract the little girl, urged her along saying "Sing Lucy, sing". And she did! That brave little Lucy Burnham grew up to be a quite exceptional woman.

Her daughter Doris has an interesting memory of Spittlesea Hospital, an isolation hospital located outside Luton and then deep in the country. This hospital took care of patients suffering from serious contagious diseases such as typhoid, cholera, smallpox and diphtheria, the killer diseases of the time. Doris tells of her experience when she was around 14 years old and was then the youngest patient to be admitted to Spittlesea. She was working at Kent's when the diphtheria epidemic struck the town, during which time about 30 people from Kent's alone went down with the disease.

She had always suffered with throat infections and on this occasion the doctor was called out and duly took swabs from her nose and throat. At this time Doris remembers, during the First World War, it was necessary to billet soldiers out in private houses whilst they were being trained. On this occasion Doris was not in bed although very poorly, but was wrapped up and sitting in a corner whilst the family played cards with the soldiers who were billeted on them. At this point the ambulance or conveyance from Spittlesea called at the house to take Doris to the isolation hospital, the swabs having confirmed diphtheria. The medical attendant was appalled to find Doris not only out of bed but sitting up, this being considered very dangerous for diphtheria patients, who were made to lie flat in bed. So Doris was taken off to the hospital where patients stayed approximately one month or even more while swabs were taken at regular intervals until they were clear of the disease. Being her mother's child, Doris overcame diphtheria with the same determination that her mother overcame her crushed hand and tells of several people dying whilst she was there. The epidemic attacked the young people first at this time and later spread to the older population – many died in the town.

Doris remembers that visitors came to see the patients

but were only allowed to see them through a glass window – those who were up and recuperating stood by the window to see the visitors. This of course was in the time before a cure was found for diphtheria and consequently there were many deaths.'

THE DOCTOR

'If you needed medicine or ointment from the doctor, the postman would bring it to Stanbridge by bicycle, wrapped in very white paper sealed with red sealing wax.'

'In the early years of the century, the doctor for Stevington lived in Turvey, and the dentist lived next door to him. If we needed the doctor we had to walk over the fields to see him, if he was sent for he travelled by bicycle. The dentist would charge sixpence for extracting a tooth. The midwife lived locally in the village, but she also covered Bromham village.

Later the doctor used a room in one of the almshouses at Stevington. He came every Tuesday and Friday. For a house call you put a note in the box at the shop, and the same if you wanted a bottle of cough mixture or other medicine. The doctor filled the bottles from the back of his car. The doctor cost sixpence a week which was paid to Mrs Ruffle, or if you wanted slightly better treatment you belonged to the National Friendly Society.'

HOME REMEDIES

'The weekend was the start of it all. Out came the horrible pink pills, goodness knows what they were for, and the vile syrup of figs. It all had to go down, like it or not, then it was a quick run down the garden to the loo hoping the last piece of newspaper square had not been used from the string hanging on the wall. Then came the bath, an old long tin job in front of the kitchen fire, everyone jumping in one after the other with top-ups of hot water in between.

Terrible earache was treated with an onion in each ear tied round with a dirty sock and being sent to bed. I don't know how you were expected to sleep, but somehow you did and it was a sure cure. Coughs and colds were treated with a good old dollop of goose grease or camphorated oil rubbed on the chest in front of the fire (phew, the stink!). Then came boils and things. Out came the soap and sugar plaster, slapped on the offending part, and it had to stay on until all inflammation had gone down.'

'There was a resident of Stevington who made an ointment from the mallow plant for use on boils etc and she would charge sixpence for filling any size jar you took along to her. She never passed on the recipe to anyone – it died with her.'

FUNERALS

'As my grandfather was the local builder/undertaker at Sharnbrook in the 1910s my forebears were very involved with funerals! The church bell was tolled when a person died – it was evident whether it was a man or a women who had died as the bell was tolled differently. The bell tolled the age of the deceased.

My grandmother was known to weep when the bell

tolled as it was her job to make the shroud and as she had eight children to look after this was an added task for her. She made the shroud out of "dimity" and it had a large box pleat down the front, on which was sown satin buttons for a man and bows (bought) for a woman.

The coffins were made in the carpenter's shop and my mother helped my grandmother line them (bought lining) after the hot black pitch had been poured in. The outside was then polished (if damp weather the polishing was done in the house!) and then the handles put on. The children kept away when the coffins were being made as the men told them that they would be put in and the lids put on! Coffins were made for the adjoining villages of Souldrop and Bletsoe as well as for the village of Sharnbrook. They were made for a cost of 32 shillings each, but this was waived if the family couldn't afford it.

Once when the weather was snowy the men walked to Bletsoe with a coffin. One day when my grandfather was putting the corpse in the coffin upstairs his bowler hat went missing from the room downstairs!

There was a funeral procession from the house to the church with mourners walking behind the bier. Every window in all of the houses on the route would have their curtains drawn and men would stand at the roadside with their hats in their hands to show respect. My mother as a child with her brothers and sisters would peep at the procession as it went by.'

'When someone died in Stevington, curtains used to be drawn in Church Road and the children quickly taken in from the school playground. The bier was kept in the church vestry and the body would be laid out and kept in the front room of the house until the day before the funeral. A Mrs Liza Lacey did the laying out, plus bringing babies into the world and sitting with the sick. Sometimes she would ask Mrs Swain to help her with the laying out and Mr Swain always made sure Mrs Swain washed her hands afterwards – he never fancied eating that night and wouldn't eat a pudding for a week. The bell tolled three times for a man, twice for a woman and once for a child.'

TAKING THE CENSUS IN 1951

Every ten years since 1841 householders have been required to complete a census form. The difficulties in 1951 faced by those who actually collected the forms probably have not changed a great deal in those 110 years.

'In 1951 when our children were small we were living in St Michael's Road, Bedford. Money was very tight, so we jumped at the offer of £10 per person to distribute and collect Census papers in the local area.

We knew that if we both applied we would have to ask our faithful baby-minder to look after the boys – but £20 seemed a fortune to be earned for delivering and collecting a few papers. At the time we were just able to keep the little Austin Ruby car – bought with the Army gratuity – on the road and this would be an added bonus.

The areas we were to serve were Biddenham and Willington parishes, two completely contrasting villages.

One was the home base of mostly well-to-do folks and the other had an agriculturally-based population.

The mountainous stack of papers left with us seemed overwhelming, as we were required to enter addresses on each form from a prepared list, before we started our rounds. We decided when "on the beat" to share the distribution of forms in each village and assumed that we would complete Biddenham in the morning and so move on to Willington in the afternoon. We had not taken into account the number and length of front paths and drives we would have to traverse.

Starting early next morning in order to catch the housewives before they went shopping, we stopped at each house to explain that we would be collecting the completed forms on the following Monday and that the law made it compulsory to fill in the forms correctly. Some householders saw us as government representatives on whom they could grind their favourite axes. One of the longest delays was when my husband called at the Hon Romola Ruddell's house. He plodded up the long rhododendron-lined drive with the wind snatching at the forms in his hand, rang the door bell and waited. After quite an interval the door was opened by the butler in a morning suit. He listened and, half closing the door, disappeared into the nether regions. He returned to tell my husband that Lady Romola would see him in half an hour. Anxious to move on with still three quarters of the village to be visited, my husband explained that he would be collecting the form after the weekend. A dim Edwardian figure appeared from the far end of the entrance hall. She told the butler she would attend to the matter if the caller could step inside. He was ushered into a mahogany-furnished library and she invited him to sit at the table while she catechized him about filling the form in. After several hold ups like this we returned home for lunch, and finished the village that afternoon.

At Willington next day we were up against quite a different problem. We were of course calling on government business and were definitely "one of them". At one cottage door the woman set about me on the subject of "cheese rationing". "How can my husband do a day's work in the fields on the paltry allowance of cheese permitted on the ration books?" she asked indignantly. My husband met with accusations over mean "meat rations" and we could not convince these women that we had no influence on food rations. We were struggling to bring up a family under the same restrictions anyway. Finally at the end of the afternoon we were only too glad to get home and put our feet up.

The collection of the forms should have been a relatively simple matter as we knew our patch and were forewarned about vociferous house-holders and aggressive dogs. However, from early morning the wind blew and the rain bucketed down. As we collected the census forms they were snatched from our hands and blown into the ever growing puddles. Each time we opened the door of the Ruby a flurry of wind scattered the growing pile of papers, all creased and sodden.

On Wednesday we heaved a sigh of relief and nursed our aching feet, considering that the £20 we hoped we had earned was not by the sweat of our brows but by every aching muscle in our tired frames. Our self-congratulatory musings were interrupted by a knock on the front door. A young man stood waiting with a sheaf of papers in his hand. May I have your completed census forms please, he asked. "Of course," I answered, rushing into the sitting room and searching wildly through papers on the desk and behind the candlesticks on the mantlepiece. Red-faced I rushed down the passage into the kitchen. There sat the census form amongst the laundry bills and butcher's bills, as blank and innocent as the day it was delivered through the letter box.

After four days of repeated admonitions to house-holders in two Bedfordshire villages, we had completely forgotten to fill in our own.'

CHILDHOOD &
SCHOOLDAYS

DAYS OF FUN AND LAUGHTER

The freedom to wander and to explore epitomises childhood of years gone by, when games could be played in the road without fear of traffic and children could be out and about all day without undue parental concern.

A CHILD'S YEAR

'When I was a young girl in the late 1920s I lived with my father, mother and brother on a farm in a tall red bricked house, which was called Red House Farm. From the top storey, two windows looked out onto ploughed fields to the left, grass fields in the middle with ponds in them, and a big wood on the right. The main road to the village ran in between the wood and our house.

In the winter it was very cold and windy situated on top of a hill, but it was very exciting when it snowed and we could take our sledge out and slide down the steep hill, with many a spill but we never hurt ourselves.

In the spring when the lambs were born I used to help Dad look after them, and if any lost their mothers, or they had too many to rear themselves, we had to feed them by hand. This meant giving them milk from a bottle four or five times a day. From then on, they were nearly always pets and would follow us everywhere, a real nuisance sometimes.

The spring also brought primroses in the wood and

everywhere was a mass of yellow. Bluebells followed and turned the wood into a beautiful blue. Many bunches were picked and taken home to be put in big glass jam jars.

Hay time followed, when horses and carts were used to bring the hay home and it was built into big stacks ready for winter to feed the cattle and sheep.

The next time we looked forward to was the school holidays, when we had six long weeks and warm sunny weather. It also brought the harvest work, and my brother and I had to drive the horses and carts back and forth to the fields to fetch the corn home. Some harvests would take longer than others, it all depended on the weather. I can remember some years when the ruts were filled with water and then we had to wait until it all dried up again. After the ricks had settled down, two men came from the village to thatch them to keep them dry all through the winter.

By this time the nuts were getting ripe in the wood, and we took our baskets and filled them to the brim. These we put in a cupboard by the fire to dry, ready to be eaten round the fire in the winter.

When the days grew shorter we had to stay indoors, and we played games such as snakes and ladders, ludo and snap. We also had nice story books to read.

Christmas was a time we looked forward to. One year an aunt and uncle arranged for all our cousins to come to a party, held in our house because we had a very large room. After tea and games, they produced a very large cracker and my cousin and I had to pull this and when we did manage to get it apart all the contents fell on the floor, and there was a mad rush to pick up a present, they were worth having in those days, and everyone went home very happy.'

'My family lived in Church End, Biddenham, a small village just west of Bedford. I remember long summer days when the village women went pea picking for Mr Rawlins, a local farmer, and we children helped a little and played in the field. We went gleaning after harvest to collect corn for the chickens.

Sunday school treats were a highlight when we would have races and a lovely tea and prizes for the best attendance for the year. The afternoon ended with the children scrabbling for sweets. Mother was one of the founder members of Biddenham WI and they gave Christmas parties for the children of members.

I remember swimming in the river in summer and skating on the pond in winter, and tobogganing down the slopes; also avoiding the hundreds of frogs when they were crossing from one pond to another to mate. My elder brother would sometimes push me round on a truck wearing a blindfold and I had to try to guess where in the village I was.

I would fetch milk from the farmer straight from the cow, and call at the pub for vinegar for Mother to pickle vegetables. I used to visit Mr and Mrs Billing who lived in a thatched cottage by the war memorial. Mr Billing always wore a smoking jacket and little round cap, and his wife gave me very thinly sliced bread spread with salted butter, which was a great treat. She once allowed me to play their harmonium. When the old lady died I was given her work box to remember her by.'

'After school a bunch of us children at Stevington would race to the local baker's to see if he had baked us a little loaf. He would do this with the dough left over from the day's baking. We would then share this around.

We had a station in those days. Saturday trips to Bedford meant a walk to the station and the journey in by train, making one stop at Oakley. It took about a quarter of an hour. I used to travel to Luton every day to school – I left on the 7.38am train and returned home at 5pm.

There was no battling then with the supermarket trolley. You filled in your order in a notebook and dropped it in to the local store and your order would be delivered to your door. Have we progressed? Of course, when rationing was on we children could not go and buy sweets at any time.

At harvest time we would go to watch a field of corn being cut along with other spectators. The binder would start at the outside and go round the field, gradually working towards the middle. When there was just a small area left the rabbits would run out and there would be men with guns shooting them. After the corn had been put into stooks to dry out it would be carted away and I would go with my mother, brother and sister along with other mothers and children to glean. We would pick up the ears of corn with stalks of six inches or so and, keeping all the ears neatly together, pick until your hand was nearly bursting! Then mother tied it up with string and this was put into a basket and taken home to feed the hens. The stubble in the field was about three to four inches high which scratched your ankles to pieces and stung like mad in your bath that night.

In June/July every year we would go on a family walk on a Sunday night to get wild strawberries. The best ones grew on the railway embankment near Winsey Wood and we would come home with lots but with very dirty ankle socks!

On Good Friday a whole band of people used to go up to the woods to pick primroses and violets to decorate the church for Easter Sunday. The altar flowers would be bought, but the rest were wild flowers or those picked out of the garden.'

'After school at Woburn was time for apple scrumping in the butcher's garden, then at lambing time we went to the farm to collect lambs' tails (which the farmer cut off in those days) for a tasty dinner when singed. The butcher's slaughterhouse was, we thought, a great place, where we tugged on the rope to pull the beast's head down on the block to be pole axed, at first not daring to look, but as we got braver, thought nothing of it. Our parents did not have to tell us about the birds and the bees. It was nature in the raw down the butcher's yard.'

THE GAMES WE PLAYED

'Our games were played in the streets, fields, school playgrounds or each other's homes. They involved much running, hopping, skipping, jumping, climbing, calling and shouting. We bowled hoops in the road, bounced balls by walls, and made dreadful slides like black glass

116

on icy footpaths. In the 1920s we could play safely in the streets, there was so little traffic.

There were ring games, – Lucy Lockett, Farmer Wants A Wife, Poor Sally Sits A-Weeping, Sally Go Round The Moon, Ring of Roses. There was Oranges and Lemons, A-Hunting We Will Go, Sheep, Sheep Come Over and The Good Ship Sails. There were games for sides, like Nuts in May, Hopping Cockerels, and Three Old Men Come Workhouse, my favourite. After sides were chosen by means of one of our numerous "counting out" rhymes one side advanced to the middle of the road and announced "Three Old Men Come Workhouse". "What's your trade?" we were asked. "All sorts and all sizes," we replied. "Then show us." Then we had to mime the trade we had decided on, and if it was guessed, we had to turn and run to avoid being caught.

We had different games in different seasons, never deviated from. There was whip and top time, "fag-cards" which we expertly flicked to lie over our opponent's, when we could claim them both. Marbles, dark red or green ones, 20 for a penny, but they were made of clay and broke easily. A glass one from a lemonade bottle was a treasure, and we rarely "played" them. We had skipping-rope time, either skipping with long ropes twirled by volunteers, or with our own wooden-handled ones. Salt, Pepper, Vinegar, Mustard we chanted, skipping like fury when we got to Mustard. We also "Bowed to the King, Curtseyed to the Queen, and Turned our Backs on the Kaiser" all while we were skipping.

We played Mob Stick, where as many as possible tried to jump on the back of the unfortunate boy bending head down to a wall, and we played hopscotch and jackstones, using small pebbles if we had no bought set of stones.

In the summer holidays, perhaps 20 or 30 of us would set up a street fair, chalking out pitches on pavements, and bringing out treasures and little games. Peep-shows, cigarette card albums, which were mines of information, skittles, jackstones and ring boards, bagatelle boards, dolls and dolls houses (shoe box variety), pea shooters and stilts. We charged a pin, button or cigarette card a go, and sometimes grown-ups would give us a halfpenny.

In winter we played Tick, Hide and Seek, and Stag, making a lamp-post our base. There was a version called I Ackey, said to be a corruption of the Latin "hic jacet", "here I lie", and we lay hidden until the catcher spotted us and called our name and hiding place when we had to come out and go back to base.

We also played Cat and Stick. The cat was a short thick stick sharpened at each end to lethal points. It was hit sharply on one end with the stick, and it jumped into the air, whereupon you gave it an almighty whack, and sent it flying down the road.'

'Us children played all sorts of games in those far off days, each in their season. Whips and Tops meant trying to see who could keep up the longest. First the top had to be spun before you could whip it. Tops came in different shapes and sizes. Whips were a straight stick with a length of string or if you were lucky a piece of boot lace, leather of course. Bowling hoops along with a stick was another favourite. Hoops were wooden or in a few cases iron, if one was lucky enough to find one in the blacksmith's rubbish.

In hopscotch a chalk oblong divided into numbered squares was drawn on a spare piece of ground. The aim was to hop and push the pitcher, a flat flint stone, from square to square without touching the lines and starting in a different square at every turn. If you had a good round, next time you slid your pitcher in the next square to start a new round.

Skipping was a great summer pastime, the rope being stretched across the road with a turner at each end. There was no limit to the number of rhymes we skipped to, the rope turning ever faster for salt, mustard, vinegar, cayenne, pepper.

All sorts of ball games were played up any empty wall – sixes, sevens, twelves, donkey and crawley ball, the ball being thrown and bounced in various ways. French Cricket was played with a cricket bat and tennis ball, football and cricket with a soft ball.

Chasing games were a must; Tig, High Cock A Roney, and chasing each other round the shrubbery outside the pub and round the "green thing", the green thing being an electrical installation on waste ground. Great fun.

We went fishing and paddling in the brook. The fishing tackle was a long stick, and on it was tied a length of string complete with cotton reel float, bent pin hook and garden worms as bait. We caught tiddlers though. Tree climbing was an adventure, not to be recommended to the timid.

Winter came with snowballing and sliding on puddles and ponds. One never to be forgotten year of joy the brook froze solid tempting even the grown ups to try its slippery surface. Tracking in the winter evenings was a form of Hide and Seek with a false trail being laid to mislead the seekers, though how we saw it in those dark early evenings is a childhood secret.'

'Few entertainments existed in those days and children at Thurleigh amused themselves with games such as hopscotch, top and whip, hoop and five stones. Hopscotch was drawn out in the middle of the road with a piece of limestone, and if a motor vehicle did appear – they were few and far between before the Second World War – we simply picked up our stones and stood to the side of the road while it passed. Top and whip was another game played in the middle of the road.'

'Children's games in Dunstable included spinning tops, marbles, five stones, statues, tig (or tag), flicking (or skimming) cigarette cards and milk bottle tops (the cardboard ones), pee-wee (a game played with two sticks), skipping and hoops. Games all used to be played "in season".'

HONEY AND FLIES

'The baby screamed. George retrieved the dummy from the sand heap. He wiped it on the back of his short trousers, where there was already a sticky wet patch from previous wipings. The wasps were shooed away from the open honey pot and the dummy used to stir in a few flies that had lingered too long. The baby smiled. He was used to the grit, honey and insect mixture. We went back to playing our hopscotch in the road undisturbed by traffic.

The long summer holiday stretched before us, hot and dry; the last one of peace in our young lives, though we knew nothing of that then. The boys wandered off to the Pightle to kick a ball of old rags about. Us girls went to the old stone pits to make our houses under the bushes. The baby sprawled asleep in the pram. We picked wild flowers and put them in a little paste jar collected from the rubbish heap. Blue flowers were smashed to pulp and smeared on the baby's face, to cure his impetigo. His mother never noticed this addition to the gentian violet she applied. We longed to get ringworm in our hair, because, rumour had it, "the doctor would electrify your head, all your hair would fall out, when it grew again it would be curly".

Hunger forced us home and we ran down the lane, the pram leaping and crashing on the uneven ground. Over it went and the baby flew through the air. We stumbled and fell to the ground, grazing our knees. Everyone cried. More grit and honey quietened the baby and the thought of iodine on our wounds quietened us. We mopped up the blood with already grey hankies and decided that if we kept quiet, no one would notice.

The penny knotted in the corner of my hanky reminded me that the church fete started at two o'clock. Children got in free. I headed for the White Elephant stall. There was a cross, about an inch long, made from carved bone. In the centre was a piece of glass and by putting this to my eye, I could see a picture. My penny was refused; twopence was the price. The lady serving on the stall decided that she would buy it herself. I was grief stricken and bought a brooch of slightly damaged mosaic, showing a classical scene, for my penny. Traffic free roads, impetigo and iodine have long gone, but my brooch lies in a drawer, reminding me of a summer in 1939, when I was six years old.'

'THE CHILDREN MUST BE OCCUPIED'

'My childhood thoughts often return to a time just prior to the Second World War.

My father was a builder and my mother ran the corner shop that was also our home in Queens Park, Bedford. The area was so named because almost all the residents were employed by the Queens Engineering Works nearby.

"The children must be kept occupied" was the continual cry of my parents, and this they did, almost too successfully. I suppose the need to keep us busy (particularly me) was because my parents were busy too. The shop never closed until 9pm then we had back door callers for sugar, milk or a packet of five Woodbine cigarettes. No-one ever appeared to be turned away.

Sundays were still busy as my father, a lay-preacher on the Methodist Circuit travelled regularly to village chapels for both morning and evening services. Along with my brother and my two sisters we attended the Moravian church Sunday school twice a day, a few doors away from home. It didn't seem like a church, it had no centre aisle, the priest was a Minister, and the service was quite like a chapel service.

During the week we were back for Scripture lessons and even sat an annual written examination for which we were awarded certificates and book prizes.

Throughout the week other activities were arranged;

Brownies, skating, elocution and pianoforte lessons, but my favourite pursuit was dancing. I attended Miss Dora Bull's Dancing Academy in Foster Street, Bedford; a small house with a small front room called a studio. It qualified for this exalted title because it had a large mirror over the fireplace and a wooden bar around the room. Ballet, National, Tap and Acrobatic dancing were all taught with at least 20 pupils in the studio, plus the piano and Miss Bull out front giving instructions. A biscuit tin was passed round for the one shilling fee to be paid by each pupil.

Once a year a dancing display was held at the Town Hall Theatre (now the Civic Theatre) and I can still remember how heavy the suitcase was, containing all the costumes (made by my busy Mum) plus shoes and accessories to complete the outfits. Although only a small girl it was quite acceptable at that time to travel to and fro on the bus all alone.

Miss Bull's students also competed in the Bedford Eisteddfod (now the Music Festival). How proud we all were to perform, and how nervously we sat through the adjudicator's remarks before the final placings were announced. I recall after one of my tap dances the adjudicator said I had "a lovely rhythm" – I hurried home to tell my mother that I had won the cup because the judge liked my (hair) ribbon.

Were they really happy days? How I longed sometimes to stay in by the coal fire in the drawing room and listen to the wireless like my school friends. I can still remember running all the way home from the various activities because I was so frightened of the dark.

Looking back I am glad my parents arranged so much for me – I am glad now that I did it all. I am still no pianist and now my arthritic joints won't allow me to skate or dance very well, but nothing learned is wasted and I can appreciate these arts when they are performed well.'

'As patrol leaders at Toddington in the 1950s, my friends and I were allowed to borrow the tent for our first taste of camping. The tent was duly pitched in an old sand pit at White Hart Farm, which belonged to Sue's parents. All our food ration was consumed while we waited for the rain to stop – it didn't. The night was long, cold and dark and it soon found us making our way across the field to the welcoming light and comfort of the farm.'

THE STRANGER

'When I was twelve years old I lived in Sandy and travelled by train every day to Bedford to the Girls Modern School in St Pauls Square. I was usually with other girls, but this particular afternoon I was on my own. I boarded an empty carriage at Bedford St Johns station to go home and a man got in and sat in the opposite corner. He was about 40 and I did not like the look of him, so I quickly got out and entered another carriage. In the 1930s all carriages were separate – no corridors.

My parents had a drapers and outfitters shop in Sandy and soon after arriving home my mother said to me, go and tell Dad tea is ready. I opened the door into the shop and to my horror the man who was in the carriage I vacated in Bedford was talking to my Dad. On seeing me, he said, "So here is the young lady who did not like the look of me". He was a commercial traveller for a haberdashery firm.'

TREATS, SWEETS AND POCKET MONEY

Outings and treats were eagerly anticipated in the days when children seldom got the chance to travel far from their home town or village. Pocket money had to be earned and sweets were often a once-a-week extravagance.

RED LETTER DAYS

'Red letter days for me were three annual events in the church calendar – the Sunday school Christmas party and especially the arrival of Father Christmas and going up to get my present from him, off the tree; the summer outing to the seaside in the train specially laid on for the occasion; and the church bazaar. What I remember about it is the lovely tea, set out on small tables, each covered with a pretty hand embroidered cloth, or one with a deep edging of hand crocheted lace. On each was a three tier cake stand, with a sponge sandwich on the top plate. Before I sat down, I always went round the tables looking for the one with the nicest sponge!

Another memorable event was the school concert, with three evening performances during the week. All the practising was done after school hours. The highlight was having our faces blackened for the American negro songs. The mothers made the brightly coloured suits and the wigs were made from old black woollen socks. Finally, there was the bun fight back stage after the last performance.'

'I left school at the age of 14. We never had a holiday when I was a child at Langford Ivel. Our red letter day was the Sunday school outing, which was usually a day at Clacton, Skegness or Wickstead Park. Another occasion we looked forward to was the Christmas party, when we were awarded a prize for our attendance at Sunday school. My sister, brother and I went every Sunday, and when we were older we went to church with my father.'

'Wymington had a ballast hole, though always spoken of as "ballist hole", and this was the rendezvous of every holiday, weekend, and summer evening walk. The approach was from footpaths and hedgerows leading out or into the village. Rabbits played there in great numbers, and minnows, tadpoles, newts and all known water plants floated between tall reeds. The reflections into deep water made spectacular shadows; think of any wild flower and it grew there, as well as mushrooms in abundance.

This was the haven for lads to learn to swim, a lido for my two brothers, no bathing suits, no towels, the sun and the wind did the necessary. Come winter this was the ice rink. The Midland Railway line overlooked this area and the train drivers and stokers would give a blast on the steam whistle, passengers waved and kids responded with happy frantic waving.

Picnics, lemonade, and natural spring water. Sunday was kept for strolling; it was a good company, George, John, Tom, and the state of the growing crops. Overhanging trees made a harbour for tail-swinging cattle, and girls went home with daisy chains.

How did we get the "Ballist Hole"? Sand was dug for the making of bridges and a mile long tunnel and the earth raised the track for the London, Midland and Scottish Railway, done manually by men and horses in the time of the Boer War.

Alas modern agriculture has destroyed this idyllic spot, but not the days of youthful memories.'

'Every Good Friday we children went primrosing. We had something to eat and drink with us and we walked from Kempston to Stagsden Woods.

As children we played games such as tag and most of us had skipping ropes, hoops and whip and top. We played ball games and leapfrog. There was no wireless or television but we did have magic lantern shows.'

'How exciting Saturdays were. The Saturday penny! My sisters and I walked to the sweetshop and eyed the array of things we could get for one penny. Bars of chocolate, aniseed balls, sherbet dabs etc – I'm sure the sherbet tasted better in those days. There were few cars about in Wootton in the 1930s and with the roads being clear we were able to play whip and top, clattering iron hoops along, hopscotch and skipping with old clothes lines!'

CHILDHOOD OUTINGS

'When Whipsnade Zoo first opened the village school teacher at Salford arranged an outing to go and see all those animals we had read about in books. We had camel and elephant rides and were fascinated by the lions, tigers, bears, monkeys and other animals.

We went to Felixstowe and Hunstanton on day trips. What a thrill that first glimpse of the sea, filling the whole horizon. Great fun was had paddling, building forts and sand castles when the tide was out, only to see them washed away when the tide came in. As the beach at Felixstowe was all pebbles we found our entertainment on the pier and at the amusement booths. The coach taking us on these day trips left the village at 6am and with a stop on the way for light refreshment we reached our destination at about 11am, leaving for home at about 6pm and again stopping on the way back to arrive home around 11pm, tired but happy.

Picnics were well remembered outings to all sorts of

places, one regular being to the sand pits at Aspley Heath a four mile walk each way. We took jam jars to fill with different colour sands to form a pattern.

Sometimes the Mothers' Union had afternoon outings to a different village and we children went with our mothers, for tea and games on some other vicarage lawn.'

EARNING MONEY

'When I started school at Millbrook in 1924 I can remember between 20 and 25 children attending. At the age of eleven they went on to school in Ampthill or Bedford. Going home we often used to visit the Boiling Pot (the village well or covered spring, known by this name because of the bubbling caused by the inflow) for a drink of clear water. In the afternoons we went to the farm at the top of the hill to collect four cans of milk for neighbours, for which we received threepence a week.'

'When I was about ten years old and still at school, I would frequently cycle to Bedford during my lunch break for my father. The round trip was 16 miles. I would be sent to Gales the local builders' merchants to fetch paint, which came in a lumpy powder form.

Before it could be used for painting this powder had to be ground to a fine powder to which was added other ingredients, depending on the type of paint it was. After school it was my job, together with my sister, to grind this powder, turning the grinding machine by hand. To pass the time we would sing hymns from a Sankey and Moody hymn book.

I had to leave school one day after my fourteenth

birthday. On the Saturday following my father bought a dozen hens for me to enable me to earn some money by selling the eggs. I used to cycle once a week to the market at St Neots about eight miles away, transporting my eggs very carefully to sell for one penny each. My mother also bought eggs from me but I had to pay for all my chickenfeed out of the proceeds, also save enough money to buy my next lot of pullets. I do not long for the return of my childhood days for all I can remember is very hard work!'

THE HAPPIEST DAYS OF OUR LIVES?

Memories of schooldays from the beginning of the century to the 1920s are of long walks to school, cold classrooms and chilblains, and the cane. Yet many children, thanks to hard working teachers, were sent out into their working lives at 14, or even younger, with a good educational grounding and, despite the drawbacks, happy memories.

SCHOOLDAYS UP TO THE GREAT WAR

'When she was four my mother went to a dame school about a mile from home. When she was six her elder sister

130

went to the Girls Modern School. The headmistress was persuaded to take mother as well. She was the youngest ever but as she could read and do sums she was accepted and soon overtook her elder sister. At first they walked the three miles to school, then after two years a bus ran holding twelve people, all children on the 8.30. There was fierce rivalry between the children attending the Bedford schools – the boys fighting and the girls not speaking to those from other schools. For lunch they would walk to Miss Dolby's house in Lansdown Road. Miss Dolby was the head. My mother hating custard and other puddings, always threw it in her handkerchief into St Paul's churchyard on the way back. When she was older she cycled to school and always had dates with the boys of Bedford School and Bedford Modern. She could have been expelled for talking to boys!'

'I remember my mother telling me that in the late 1800s they had to pay one penny a week to go to school. She could read and write, but my father couldn't.

We always wore white pinafores with frills over each shoulder. Another important item – we had two pairs of shoes each! One best for Sundays and one for school. The school ones were always leather, and every Saturday Dad used to lard the school shoes to protect them and make them waterproof and last longer. Sunday school shoes were of a cheaper kind and bought from the Universal shop in Harpur Street.

In the infants school at Stevington we had slates and chalk, graduating to books and pens in older classes. Every Friday afternoon we would have sewing classes and would always make pillow cases and aprons for the

Church Sale. We also had a school bank and my sister and I would take a penny each week; this went towards our clothes and shoes.

We had a half day off school when it was the day for the Sunday school outing. We went to church in the afternoon, followed by tea in the Church Room and finished with games and races and a scramble, when the vicar threw a box of sweets for the children to scramble for.'

'I was born in Lewis's Cottages in Wymington. My first memories are of sitting in a little hut belonging to a man named Dick Bull who was a clicker by trade. My brother and I would sit among the sacks of leather pieces as he was working from home. I started school at the age of five at Church School, Wymington. The teacher was extremely strict. In winter she sat near the lovely warm fire whilst the pupils sat shivering in their desks.

The girls in the school were often given the teacher's black stockings to darn and had to repair her bloomers and other underwear. Every playtime the farmer's wife from Manor Farm would bring a large jug of fresh milk for her two sons to drink; the rest of us looked on longing to share in this but never did.

During 1916 we had a terrible blizzard bringing down telegraph poles and trees. It was very exciting for us youngsters. Another excitement was when Mr Griggs the butcher from Rushden came to kill a pig. We were given the pig's bladder which we blew up and played football with as it was very tough.'

'Doris and her brother and sisters all attended Dunstable

132

Road school, then a new school built around 1898. They walked there and back, a distance of one and a half to two miles each way, there being no public transport at the time (the trams came to Luton in 1908).

At the outbreak of war in 1914 all the male teachers left immediately to join up and during this interruption Doris left school just before her 14th birthday. She joined her sister at Kent's making fuse caps for ammunition.'

'At the local school at Sharnbrook there were two big fires – and the headmaster always stood in front of one of them! When the children from the Colmworth estate and other distant houses reached school they were allowed to stand in front to warm themselves before lessons began. The children suffered badly from chilblains in those times. All the local children went home to dinner but children from outlying districts took sandwiches. Esperanto was taught, and a map of the world was drawn on the playground.

My mother remembers having half a day off school to pick blackberries for jam. They got threepence per pound. She also remembers going up to Winsey Farm during the war to pick linseed.'

'We had over two miles to walk to school from Moxhill Farm, Cople, and nearly half a mile down a dirty old cart track before we reached the high road so we never went to school with clean shoes in the winter time and we were often wet-footed. I remember sometimes my father would come and meet us with the pony and pig float if it was very wet in the afternoon. In the springtime we often walked home through the woods and fields and didn't get home very early as we stopped to pick primroses and

133

bluebells on the way. After I got home from school I had to help my father in the garden in the summertime and I had to help look after the pigs and sheep or go crow scaring at weekends. In the lambing season I went with my father at night to carry the lantern round the sheep yard and often the lantern used to blow out. It was one with a candle and that's all we had in those days. Often I was perished with cold.

My mother often used to sit up until twelve o'clock at night sewing and patching up clothes for us to go to school. I remember once the schoolmaster asked my brother Harry which was the original piece, as his jacket had so many patches. After some of us left school and got work things began to get a bit better.

One morning we were going to school after a storm and the ditch beside the road was full of water, about four feet deep. Well, the bigger boys began jumping over it so I thought I would have a go and I landed right in the middle. It was a very cold morning and I was soaked from head to foot. Anyway, I had to go to school in my wet clothes and when I got there the teacher undressed me and hung my clothes over the fire guard and I sat in my sister's coat until they were dry.

Our dinnertime at school was from twelve o'clock until two o'clock, so after I had my dinner I used to cut the schoolmaster's lawn. He would give me a penny a day. Then I would go straight to the shop and buy what we used to call a "lucky bag" – you mostly got sherbet or an old ring or something like that. Our teacher Miss Willsher used to practise playing the organ in church as soon as we came out to dinner, for about half an hour, and I used to go and blow the organ for her for which she gave me twopence a time, so with blowing the organ and cutting the master's lawn, I hadn't got much time to spare.

I used to get on very well with her until she made me stay in one night for about half an hour to write so many words, I don't remember what they were now. When I came out my mates were waiting for me outside the school. The teacher lived in a house on our way home so she had to pass us on the way, and as she did so she gave us a dirty look. That was the time before they had tarmac and the roads were made with granite and rolled in with a steam roller, so there were heaps of gravel beside the road. When I saw her look like that, I pulled out my catapault and a granite and I said to the others "See me hit Miss Willsher". Well, I shot this piece of granite at her. I don't know why I did it but I suppose it was on the spur of the moment. I didn't hit her but I made a big dent in the back mudguard of her bike. She came back and gave me a good telling off. I well remember it was a Friday night and she said "You wait until Monday morning when I tell the schoolmaster". All that weekend I was worried to death but anyway I went to school on the Monday morning expecting to have a few strokes of the cane. But I don't think she told him, for I never heard anything else about it. Perhaps she thought I wouldn't pump the organ for her any more!'

FLITWICK SCHOOL IN THE 1920s

'I started school at Flitwick in the year 1919 at the age of three years as did most of my contemporaries.

In those days there was no separate infants school, we all attended the old school in Dunstable Road. It was

135

some years later that the infants section of the school was transferred to a building in Station Road.

As we lived in Windmill Road we had a good mile to walk and in those days school dinners were unheard of and we all came home to have ours, which entailed a four mile walk every day so us three year olds needed plenty of stamina, especially on rainy wintry days. There were no such things as mackintoshes and wellington boots then. We mostly had a thick woollen coat if we were lucky, and the stench of those coats hanging in the school lobby on a wet morning was, in a word, pungent.

The school was cold and draughty, the only warmth coming from the large open fireplaces which were usually replenished with coal, but as the teachers always stood right in front of them, only moving away to write on the blackboard, we children seldom had much benefit from them at all.

Only the lucky ones sitting in the front row ever felt the heat and they were only there because they were the ones who usually misbehaved and the teacher needed to keep an eye on them.

I think that was when I first realised that virtue is not always its own reward, being good meant you always sat at the back of the class in the coldest spot.

Most of us suffered acutely in the winter months from chilblains both on our hands and our feet. Something else we suffered from in the summertime especially, was thirst. The school house had a well in the garden but there was no provision for the school. When there was a heatwave on, the headmaster would sometimes come round at playtime with a watering can filled with water and an enamel mug, and each child would be given a

136

drink one after the other out of that one mug. We had never heard of hygiene and anyhow we were all too thirsty to care if we had.

One memory that stands out in my mind is of a very kind lady who lived just up the road from the school in a little cottage next to a large house called Hampden Lodge (the lodge has since been demolished and replaced by Hampden Road and the cottage which was one of three has been made into one house). This lady, whose name was Mrs Harris, had a wooden table outside her kitchen door and on it she always kept a bucket of fresh water covered over with a board, with a mug beside it, and all we children from Denel End were allowed to go round her back way and help ourselves on our way to school. How welcome that always was to children who had often walked a mile under a scorching sun. That drink of water was always there for us and I often think of that lady's thoughtfulness and patience as we invariably all trooped round again on our way back home.

One thing we were not allowed to do was to cheek grown ups. Our headmaster was very strict about this and often there would be a knock on the door in the middle of a lesson and it would be someone complaining that a certain child or children had been rude to them. There was one occasion I remember well. Our local roadsweeper was a tall old man and I think the schoolchildren were the bane of his life. He was always shouting or grumbling at one or another for kicking leaves about or dropping paper down just where he had cleared the path.

One morning he came marching into the school to complain about some boys who had been rude to him.

It was his "bavour" time (elevenses you'd say now) and

he had in his hand a large chunk of Bedfordshire clanger, from which he was taking frequent bites.

The headmaster asked him to point out the culprits and he looked all round the class and taking another bite of his clanger, he pointed the rest of it at one boy and said, "He wor one of 'em and he wor another", and so on all the time, much to the delight of us children, talking with his mouth full until he had sorted out five of them. The five boys were all given one stroke of the cane and made to apologise humbly to him, then honour satisfied and still munching his clanger, he stomped out of the school and back to his road sweeping.

One of the highlights of our school year was the County Eisteddfod which was held in the Corn Exchange in Bedford. Our headmaster Mr Strickland was very proud of our school choir. For several years running we carried off the County Shield for singing, and quite a few children did well in the individual classes for singing and elocution and so on, and always after the Eisteddfod, we would have a concert when all the parents would come to hear and see their offspring sing and recite their prizewinning pieces. One year I especially remember. Our headmaster was a very energetic conductor. He always did a great deal of arm waving and this particular time he was standing on a wooden box conducting the choir through its prizewinning song, when suddenly he just went through the box.

With great aplomb he carried on conducting as if nothing had happened, while the audience fell about laughing, and my mother who was sitting near the front was so amazed at the way we children in the choir reacted. Such was Mr Strickland's discipline over us that not one of us even smiled or turned a hair. We just carried on singing right to the end, whilst he conducted in the debris of the wooden box. We wouldn't have dared to do any other! Mr Strickland was a good headmaster and well respected by everyone.

He used the cane quite often on boys who misbehaved but he hardly ever caned any of the girls, and even boys he caned quite frequently have said to me in after years that he was a good teacher and they only got what they deserved.

He had a wry sense of humour and he kept a punishment book in which he recorded every caning, and one day when I was putting it away I had a sly peep and beside some of the names he had written the comments the boys had muttered on being punished, such as "I shan't come the s'arternoon" or "I shall tell our mum", and occasionally an irate mum would come storming to the school, but not very often. Most parents merely said, "You must have deserved it or you wouldn't have got it", and some like my mum would say "Here is another one to go with it!" But on the whole our schooldays were happy days.

One other little incident stands out in my mind. Though living in the country where apples were plentiful in the summer, somehow during the winter months we rarely saw them. Only the children whose parents had eating apple trees growing in their gardens brought them to school for their playtime break.

I can remember watching one of them munching away at his apple with about a dozen other boys standing round him eagerly watching and all of them chanting, "Gie us the core", and when he nearly got to it he looked round at them all and said calmly "There ain't gonna be no core", and proceeded to make sure there wasn't. These were the post war years of high prices and low wages and this small incident does highlight the hunger some of those children must have felt.

I well remember one morning when there was great excitement. We were all taken out of school and down past the blacksmith's shop and on past the old village pond (long since gone) and on up the hill to what is now Townfield Road, but then was still agricultural land, and there we all stood and watched in wonderment as the first airship to be made at Cardington sailed majestically over our heads. The headmaster said to us "Children, note this moment well. You are watching history being made".

Of course in the years that followed, we got quite used to seeing them floating in the sky until that day when the ill-fated airship the R101 crashed on a hillside in France. After that we saw them no more.

I thoroughly enjoyed my schooldays and the day I left was one of the saddest days of my life.'

VILLAGE SCHOOL LIFE

'One of my earliest childhood memories is of the day I started school at the age of five. I remember crying when my mother left me. One of the first things we did, and I recall this very vividly, was making chairs by sticking pins into conkers. We used to have a mug of Horlicks every lunchtime. One of our favourite games in the playground was skipping. We had a long rope with a child at each end, and someone would skip in the

140

middle, usually to a rhyme. One of our favourites was "salt, mustard, vinegar, pepper" with the rope getting faster all the time.

I was at the local village school where I live at Langford until I was eleven, when we went on the bus to a secondary school. We had to start wearing a uniform then, navy gymslip, white blouse, navy jumper and tie.'

'I was born in the village of Tingrith some 68 years ago. The village had a school which was attended by all children under the age of eleven. The school was run by a Miss Strudwick and she lived with her sister in a cottage that was attached to the rear of the school.

A bell was rung by pulling a rope each day to tell us what time to be there. If anyone was late, they had to have a very good reason or else they were for it. The school was heated by an open fire and I can remember having to get there early to clean the ashes and light the fire before school began. (The cinders were kept to help get the fire going.) During the winter months we were allowed to sit around the fire when we had finished our main lessons. The younger children sat in the front and the older ones at the back. All children from five to eleven were in the same class.

The school was a church school so the vicar often came to see us. He was a very large man and when the boys had been playing about in the street he would come and complain in front of the whole class.

At eleven the children went to school at Westoning, three miles away. No transport was laid on to take you, you had to walk come rain, shine, hail or snow.'

'I was about eleven years old, in the 1920s, when our teacher gave us an essay to write about our village. Having heard my father say that we might be having electricity in the village within the next ten years, I wrote that in my essay. The headmistress read it to the class and tore it up, saying "Not in your time or mine!"

Worse was to come. I do not remember the subject, but I know I wrote that men would be walking on the moon in the 1980s. Another humiliation, she made all the class laugh at my essay and that also went in shreds.

The said teacher lived to see the electricity in the village, but not the landing on the moon.'

'I started on this great adventure of school in January 1929 wearing ordinary clothes and brown button boots halfway to the knee. How I envied the few in shoes but shoes for me were Sunday wear.

The village school at Salford, presided over by one teacher for pupils aged five to eleven, consisted of one room with a platform at one end. On this reposed the piano and sometimes naughty children were made to stand alone on the platform in front of the whole class as a punishment.

Adjoining this room was a lobby with rows of pegs each side to hold hats and coats. At break times we had to play in the road, not having a playground until the early 1930s. The playground was gravel being formerly part of the teacher's garden and nearby field. In the playground was a large elm tree. What fun playing chasing round it. Of course the toilets were bucket-under-the-seat jobs; boys at the front, girls at the rear.

Older pupils took it in turn to pull the school bell

summoning us to school each morning. After the register was called, this being a Church school, a hymn was sung and prayers said. Then it was "Blow your noses children" and if a hanky had been forgotten the miscreant was sent home to fetch one – if the teacher believed the plea, "Miss, I forgot my hanky" was genuine!

Tables came next, all twelve recited parrot fashion and remembered to this day. Next the daily scripture lesson followed by arithmetic, sums being set according to age and ability. Other subjects were taken more or less all together. Twice a week boys did drawing while girls did needlework.

If anyone merited the cane, the culprit had to fetch it from the cupboard where the text books were kept and hand it to the teacher before punishment on the hand was administered.

School was not all work. We played indoor games around Christmas time: Farmer's in his Den, Oats and Beans and Barley, Poor Jinny is a-weeping, etc. Sir Roger de Coverley was executed on these occasions to the tune "Keel Row". A song we sang at Christmas time had the chorus "Clap clap for Santa Claus, clap clap away, don't forget the Salford Road on Christmas Day."

Our Christmas decorations were made from bits of coloured tissue paper folded to look like flowers and sewn onto twigs (very effective) and placed in jars on the piano, teacher's desk and the mantelpiece above the open coal fire.

The school was visited each week by the rector Canon Scott in his cycling gear and once a year an Inspector came and tested us on religious knowledge.

143

On days when the Oakley Hunt met outside the pub opposite, we were allowed to lean over the school wall and watch the gathering. What fun we had trying to spot local bigwigs in a different guise.'

SCHOOLDAYS
IN THE 1930s & 1940s

Parents sending their children to school in the years leading up to and through the war would have been hard pressed to find significant changes since their own days at the village school. The Second World War, of course, brought problems of its own, particularly as lessons were disrupted by air raid warnings and schools tried to cope with an influx of young evacuees.

WITH MIXED FEELINGS

'School days are remembered with mixed feelings. There was much stricter discipline than now. Hands were inspected for cleanliness, girls had to have their hair pulled back. Swimming was performed in knitted costumes and sports were done in borrowed plimsolls because they were in such short supply. Pupils sat at desks in rows. Each desk had an ink well which would be filled afresh each day by the "ink monitor", a position of some status. Fresh milk was provided every day in third of a pint bottles.'

'I started school in 1930 at Wootton. An early memory is of being taught to knit, and having my fingers tapped with a ruler for the finished result of moss-stitch instead of rib. At the "big school" (seven to eleven years) we girls wore navy gymslips, white blouses and black stockings. From eleven to 14 years we went to senior school at Stewartby, by bus. Children from other surrounding villages also attended this school. I left school at the age of 14, just before the outbreak of the Second World War in 1939. The blackout came into force immediately on the outbreak of war, with wardens on duty looking for any chink of light. It was eerie seeing the searchlights sweeping the sky – quite frightening too.'

'At Stevington a high wooden fence separated the boys' and girls' playgrounds and they entered by different doors, only mixing for gym. The girls played rounders in the field opposite during the summer and the boys each had a little piece of ground in the school garden which they tended. A little woman called Miss Wrigglesworth was headmistress for a time and she frequently boxed children's ears for mistakes and thought nothing of caning boys as big as her. Nevertheless, when she died suddenly, aged only 34, it was a great shock to the whole village. When her funeral cortege began its journey to Kidderminster, blinds in the cottages were drawn and the church bell tolled. The schoolchildren lined the route, with the boys standing at the salute and the girls with bowed heads.

The "kiddie-catcher" was a Mr Aylott who would come with his wife on a tandem to see who was away. Lord Ampthill was one of the school governors and he visited the school twice a year.'

'We moved to Bromham in 1939 and lived on the Stagsden Road. Each day seemed packed with excitement. Water was fetched from the pump outside and we had no electricity upstairs and took a nightlight to bed with us. I was taken to school at five years old by the Rose sisters, crying all the way until a large Mr Southam at the garage told me to "Shut up child!". We had to walk home for dinner every day. I loved the milk in the little bottles, for which we had to pay tuppence ha'penny a week. Miss Markham was the headmistress and Miss Walton with bright red frizzy hair the other teacher. She cycled from Stagsden. I was terrified of them both and they seemed very old to my eyes. Storytime in the park around an old tree trunk was a delight and the magic of the old saucepan man stories were to be lived over and over.'

TOWARDS AND THROUGH THE WAR

'There were two schools in the village of Houghton Regis. One was a council school and the other a Church of England school. I went to the C of E one which was situated on the edge of the village green where we were allowed to play – weather permitting. If not, we played in our playgrounds which were separated by a brick wall – one for girls and infants, the other for boys. The toilets were at the far end of the playground. Our school was heated by an open fire which had a large fireguard. In the morning break we had Horlicks to drink which cost three pence per week. It was made by the headmaster in a large urn at the front of the classroom while we quietly got on with our work. When we were in the top class, we took turns to wash the urn in a large sink in the cloakroom.

On Ash Wednesday and Ascension Day, being a church school, we used to attend church in the morning and then go back to school for our Horlicks. Then we talked about why we had been to church and sometimes had a story read to us. We were then allowed the afternoon off school, which we would spend standing outside the council school so that we could gloat over the children when they came out to play.

Just beside our school were kennels where the hunting hounds were kept. If they were being exercised while we were playing on the green we were allowed to stroke them. They used to enjoy running about with us, but the kennel man just had to whistle and they immediately ran to him. If there was a Meet when we were at school, we were allowed to go outside to see them go off for the hunt.

Until 1935 there was no senior school in the area, and the children stayed at the same school until they were 14 years old when they left to go to work. The year I was to go to senior school was 1939 so we had to have three weeks extra holiday because war was declared and the corridors of the school had to be reinforced with sandbags and a dug-out built. At first we used to go home for mid-day dinners, walking about a mile and a half each way, but when there was more danger from bombing, we were allowed to stay at school and take sandwiches

147

to eat. The only children to have school dinners lived two miles or more away, although later it was changed so that all children could have school dinners. Our education was often disrupted by air raid practice, which we only had to use in reality a few times. Our male teachers were called up for service and we were always having our teachers changed. Many of them came from London with the evacuees.'

'There goes the air raid warning – good – now we can stop lessons! Teacher Miss Dunmore requests that we all file out quickly and quietly to the cloakrooms. In our ignorance, or should it be innocence, we all think it is good fun. We all settle down to hear another instalment of *Wind in the Willows*. When the all clear finally goes we all go back to class with our gas masks on our backs. It was very difficult to try and concentrate on the disrupted maths lesson after an air raid.

Easter was always a time to look forward to at Harrold school as Mrs Canvin the Bedford butcher's wife always brought us an Easter egg until sweets were rationed, then we had a record of The Teddy Bears' Picnic. Spring saw us all dancing round the maypole, with Miss Negus in charge – woe betide any pupil getting out of step. Summertime lessons were often given under the silver birch tree. Nature walks were a joy. We often walked across the fields to Odell (now the country park) to see an old hornbeam tree. Wild flowers were brought in as they appeared in the hedgerows and meadows, pressed and mounted in a scrapbook. I have never forgotten the names of flowers and trees thanks to those wonderful nature lessons.

When you arrived in Miss Coleman's class you thought you were cock of the walk. We had to get down to serious work now ready for the eleven-plus exam to be taken in Bedford. Our proud possession was our saving book; sixpence per week, if you were lucky, to help the war effort. We also frayed all sorts of scraps of soft material for pillows for wounded soldiers' heads. Fraying lessons were popular as we could talk during this period. Some very funny garments were knitted in our effort to do our bit. The best results were long scarves, we could hardly go wrong there.

I have very happy memories of Harrold school and its fine teachers. I now realize what a worry it must have been to have so many children, the village children's numbers swelled by evacuees, to be responsible for during wartime. We children never realized the dangers, school was just a wonderful place to be in. I thank God that we were all so fortunate to have come through those hard times so well.'

'We were four friends that did most things together, school, chapel, guides. We started school at St George of England primary school in Toddington in 1946 and walked there together – no lifts in coaches or parents' cars. Our classrooms had lattice leaded windows and no real heat. We sat at double desks with hinged lids and inkwells which proved to be a hazard if you had long plaits and sat in front of a mischievous boy. One classroom had a three-quarter height stable door leading from the playground where you had to step up and bend down at the same time to enter. The toilets were a row of wooden huts in the middle of the playground – girls backing on to boys and they froze solid at the first onset of frost. Being made Milk Monitor was a prized reward for good work.

We had our annual "events" such as climbing to the top of Congor Hill on Shrove Tuesday to hear the "Witch" frying her pancakes – you really could hear them sizzle. Also on Ascension Day, after the church service, the older children were allowed to climb to the top of the church tower. Each week during the summer, we would be taken by coach to Eversholt for a swim in the rather murky water of the pool which had a slippery bottom and the odd frog or two for good measure.

So much emphasis was put on the eleven-plus. The few who "passed" went to the high school/grammar school/technical college in Luton and the remainder finished off their schooling at the secondary school. For those travelling to Luton on public transport there was the restriction of school uniforms including knickers with elasticated legs. We were also forced to wear either felt hats or berets but these were always stuffed into pockets or bags once on the bus for the homeward journey.'

THE WORLD OF WORK

FARMING AND MARKET GARDENING

There was little choice for many young boys than to follow in father's footsteps and find work on local farms or market gardens. The farming year continued much as it had for generations, until mechanisation and 'new' crops brought changes over the past 50 years.

A FARMER'S BOY

'I was born in 1898 on my father's farm. To celebrate he sent the maid to the fields with some home-made beer, no more work was done that day! He employed quite a few men as farming was very labour intensive, the farm implements all being horse-drawn then. The nearest market town was several miles away and once a week my father would go to collect cash for the wages and order the groceries which would be delivered by horse-drawn cart, together with the mail and the weekly newspaper costing a halfpenny. My mother used to bake and make bread once a week using our own wheat which had been ground by the local miller; she also churned our own butter.

I had to walk several miles to school where we used slates and chalk; the teacher's wages were paid by the local squire. I worked on the farm until I was old enough to enlist to fight in the Great War in the machine gun

corps. I was wounded near the end of the war and returned to England on the hospital ship *Carisbrooke Castle*, to a hospital in North Wales. I was invalided out and sent home by train, arriving at a nearby station in the small hours of the morning where the postman saw me struggling and helped me home. I resumed working for my father, when the farmworker's wage was £1 per week, until I married and bought my own farm in Little Staughton.

THE FARMING YEAR

'After I left school in 1916 I worked with my father on the farm at Cople. I was nearly always with the horses, of which I was very fond. I used to drive the horses for ploughing or drilling corn. When we went to drill we had four horses, two in front and two behind, and I drove them with one rein. If you didn't turn round properly at the ends of the field you would get swore at or perhaps a lump of dirt thrown at you, I've had it many a time. Sometimes when we were out ploughing it would rain nearly all day and we got wet through – we had no wellingtons or plastic macs. We dried our boots out beside the kitchen fire at nights and in the morning they were so stiff you could hardly get them on. We hung our coats up in the stable and put them on again next morning still wet as there was nowhere to dry them, only the kitchen stove and there was no room there with eight in the family besides Mother and Father.

We went out in the fields with the horses at seven in the morning, before it was light in the wintertime. We took our breakfast with us and the nosebags for the horses. When it was very cold we used to make a fire beside the hedge and often it would take half your breakfast time to get it going when the wood was wet so we didn't have much time to eat. We only had half an hour for breakfast from half past nine to ten o'clock and I can remember the boss coming round and saying "Was you late stopping, it's two minutes past ten." I don't know what they would say now.

We got home for dinner at three o'clock and I used to look forward to going home and having a ride on the horse's back as I was getting a bit tired by then. We had an hour for dinner, then after dinner we had to look after the horses. The horsekeeper used to feed the horses and clean them down. Often if they had been sweating a lot they would wipe them down with a wisp of straw and sometimes in the morning their hair would be matted together, and when combed down there would be plenty of dust. My job as stable boy was to clean out the stables, fetch in straw and hay and pump the water, as we had no running water then. The pipes ran through the cow yard to the horse trough and sometimes if you didn't watch it the cowman would turn his tap on so you pumped his as well, not a very nice trick to play on one.

I used to carry the hay and straw from the rickyard. We had to tie the straw in bundles as there were no bales then, and the hay I used to cut off the stack with a

154

big hay knife. We would cut a lump about a yard square sometimes, down a ladder from the top of the stack, and it was very heavy as I was only twelve when I started and I wasn't very big, but it was no use complaining, you just had to do it.

I liked the springtime best of all. It was very welcome after a rough winter. We used to cut about 200 acres of hay because we had about 100 milking cows besides a lot more following on. We had to use two machines with two horses each and that was very hard work for them when it was very hot. I've seen sweat dripping on the ground and when you got home to dinner at night the horses were too tired to feed, they only wanted to drink. It was hard work stacking the hay when I first started. It all used to be turned by hand with rakes and pitched on the carts with forks and that was hard, but before that it was dragged into rows with a horserake and sometimes we used to cock it, which meant putting it into heaps so it was easier for the men to pick up.

At first I used to drive the horses up the rows of hay while they were being loaded and when I got a bit older I had to drive them to the stack in the rickyard. You had one driver for three carts, so when you took the loaded one to the stack you would take the empty one back to the field, so there was one each end and one on the way. It's all different now. It's all cut and baled which makes it much easier and it's all picked up by tractors and mostly put into dutch barns, not like the old stacks we used to put up in the rickyard which had to be thatched. That was a very skilled job if done properly.

In the winter we had to cart the hay up to the dairy for the cows, not a very nice job loading loose hay when the

155

wind was blowing. We sometimes had to go to the top of the stack and start a fresh cut and it would be covered in frost or snow and very cold.

I think harvest time was the time I liked best, although it was very hard work. First we had to mow gangways round the outside of the fields so the horses and binder could get round without treading on the corn. That was a hard and hot job when you were beside a big hedge and couldn't feel a breeze. Then we used to tie the corn up by hand and stand the sheaves up against the hedge out of the way of the horses and binder. We used about a dozen bits of straw to make a band and I could tie up a sheaf in about two seconds. I can remember the old reapers cutting corn. They were used before the binder but they didn't tie it up, they used to have sails more like windmills with wooden pegs in them and they would sweep the corn off the platform into rows which had to be tied by hand. I never used one of them but I once saw one at work.

Then came the binder which tied up the sheaves very tidily. We always had three horses on the binder and changed them every three hours as it was very hard work. We kept on till dark, then it was home and feed and clean the horses, and up at about five the next morning to feed and clean them again to start another day.

We had two horses hitched to a pole and strapped up on their collars, then we had one in front which the boy used to ride. I did that for a few years then I used to ride the binder. I thought I was good then. When we had finished the field we had to shock it; in some counties they call it stooking, that is, stacking about a dozen sheaves together with the corn at the top. We did that from seven in the morning until eight at night day after day until it was all set up, if the weather was good. I have known the wheat to start growing in the shocks on a wet season and we had to go and turn them round so they could dry out.

Carting the corn was the same as carting the hay but a bit easier as it was all tied up. We had three carts and one driver if we were near the rickyard and four carts and two drivers if we were further away. At first I used to drive the horses from shock to shock while they were being loaded but afterwards I drove up to the stack and back. When you brought your empty cart back to the field you had to draw it up against the loaded one so the man who had loaded the cart could slide down into the empty one without getting on the ground and was ready for loading again. If you didn't draw up the cart just right you would get a good telling off.

They always built stacks side by side and left enough room in between to get a thrashing drum in so they could thrash two stacks without moving. When the corn was all stacked you did the same as you did for hay and thatched it in till the winter, when the steam engine would come to thrash it out.

I think I have done every job when we've been thrashing. My first job was to carry the water in two buckets down the rickyard to the engine, then I went to pulling out the cavins and chaff from under the drum. You had to be there all the time or it would get blocked up and if the wind was the wrong way the dust was enough to blind you, but it had to be done and it was mostly a boy or an old man that did it. You didn't grumble because there was a lot more men

157

who would have been glad of a few weeks' work, however rough.

After I finished with that job I went on top of the drum cutting the bands. Then when I was about 17 I had to cart the corn away from the drum. We put it in 18 stone sacks and six sacks went in a cart. It took two of us to lift them in and then I had to take them to the barn and carry them in and stack them up in rows, one on top of the other. I often had a sore back through carrying so many. We left a little space between the rows so the cats could get in between them and keep the mice away.

At harvest time we did a month's work from six in the morning to eight at night for an ordinary week's pay, then at the end of the month we used to have another four weeks' pay for all the overtime. Then the men would have a day off work and go to town and buy boots and clothes for the winter. They used to call that "largering day", I never did know why, and they usually had plenty of beer. I have known them to have only one pair of boots to work and go out in – they used to wash them and put blacking on them for the weekends.

After hay time and harvest we used to have the steam ploughing engines. One engine stood at each end of the field and they pulled the plough across the field with a big wire rope which wound round a big drum under the engine. Before the engines came I had to cart the coal round the fields and put it in little heaps about 30 yards apart, then when the engine driver got to them he picked it up and put it in the coal bunker. My job was to cart the water to the engines, with two horses on the water cart. It was all right the first time but when the plough went back across the field you had all the rough ground to take your water cart over. I had to pump the water by hand out of the pond and it took nearly an hour to pump the cart full. You had to keep on until dark and if you weren't there by six the next morning they would be blowing their whistles for water. The engine workers used to live in a caravan which they took with them from farm to farm and they only went home at weekends. I remember the next set of engines to come were the old steam engines converted to diesel, with the radiator where the chimney used to be, and there wasn't any coal or water to cart, which was much better as most of the engine drivers were not very pleasant people.'

'My parents were alive in 1891 and they remembered the extremely hard winter of that year all their lives. For six weeks, three in December followed by another three in the following January, it was the coldest ever experienced. The river Ouse was frozen at least 18 inches, much to the delight of skaters of all ages all day and moonlit nights, when hot coffee in hayboxes was taken to parties having fun. But indeed it was no fun for the poor farm workers and there was great poverty within the cold cottages. Children went gathering sticks and wood, no money for coal, no unemployment pay or allowances, and few had savings from the meagre wages earned by the parents. In the summer the men worked very long hours, hay making and harvest, horsekeepers started work at 5am and often laboured until dusk. Women helped with the hay, harvest, and potatoes.'

'Many men at Thurleigh worked on the farms earlier this century. To regard these men as simple yokels was an absolute injustice, men who rose early, walked to work and practised skills such as hedge laying, ditching, rick building and rick thatching. Most of the same men had a sound knowledge of handling sheep, cattle and horses, and they were fiercely proud of their straight furrows and neat stacks.'

'Several Salford village men were employed on farms in the 1930s, to milk cows, look after horses, pigs, poultry and sheep. Farm work was hard, working outside in all weathers. All the work was done manually with horses being used to pull the plough, carts, mowing and reaping machines.

After cutting, the hay was left in the field to dry. During this period it was turned once and then tedded into heaps ready to be picked up, carted away and stacked. Sheaves of corn were stooked and left in the field before being stacked in similar fashion. Some stacks were made in fields but the usual practice was to build them in the rickyard near the farm. Of course all stacks had to be thatched to keep them intact, another job done by hand (craftmen's work).

Later on the corn was threshed by the travelling thresher, whose machine again needed the assistance of a horse. The corn was stored in two cwt sacks in the granary. The straw was stacked to be used for animal bedding. Extra help was taken on for the haymaking and harvesting.

Of course cows were milked by hand. In the summer they lay in the fields and had to be fetched and taken back twice daily for the milking sessions but in winter cows were kept inside at night. Cow houses had to be mucked out daily. The muck from byres and stables was spread on the land to promote crop growth, usually a wet day job.

In late spring the sheep were sheared. Before the shearing the sheep were dipped in a chemical solution in an artificial pond, to make sure the fleeces were free from lice and sheep ticks.'

'The parish of Whipsnade had five working farms years ago, now there is only one. Haymaking and harvest were a children's delight, watching the selfbinder, cutter, and the stacking of sheaves into stooks to dry. No combine harvester then, just the farm horse and cart. But what fun! Hay rides, building of ricks, and those breaks for a ploughman's sandwich and mug of tea. Were those days always sunny? I like to think so.

What excitement when Mr Falkner's threshing machine arrived from Leighton Buzzard to be worked by Mr Jack Gravestock. Stoking the engine with hard black coal reminded the boys of trains from far away. It seemed that not a single ear of corn was wasted – golden grains into bags – what magic!

Although it was fun for us children, it had been hard graft for the farm workers, ending a long year of toil. First the ploughing and sowing, then waiting for the first glimpses of green. Then hoping for long, dry, sunny days to turn the corn to gold. Weeds were contained then without the use of chemicals. How beautiful it was to see red poppies, ox eye daisies, clover and many other wild flowers, year after year.'

'Horses were still in use on the farm at Colesden and smallholdings at Roxton in the 1940s. A few of the larger farmers owned a wheeled or crawler tractor. Mr Will Addington was one of the last farmers to have a team of cart horses to use at harvest time. Four horses were needed in a "set" for a gang of men to use, bringing the corn harvest from the fields to be stacked. Before I left Sandy school, during our summer holidays, I drove a cart, taking the empty cart out to a field and bringing a loaded one back to the stack, from seven in the morning to eight at night, or four o'clock on Saturdays, for the princely sum of one shilling per week.'

FIFTY YEARS OF CHANGE

'When I came to Studham in 1948 it was a rural village with quite a farming community. There were seven farms each with a dairy herd, and this gave employment to between four and eight people at each farm.

The cows had to be milked each morning and evening. Every morning the milk churns (which held ten gallons) were picked up by a lorry which arrived between 7am and 9am to be taken to the dairy. Each churn would have a "tie on" label with the farmer's name and the amount of milk. This was all added up and a receipt given. This was kept to check that our monthly payment was correct.

The cows were chained and each had a trough in which they were given half to three ladles of food according to the stage of their lactation. There were calves to feed, which was mainly the job of the womenfolk who were supposed to have a great deal of patience when it came to feeding calves from a bucket.

A day's work for everyone consisted of cleaning out the cowsheds, washing them down and then putting down beds of straw in the winter. The cows had to be fed with kale, mangolds, and hay which were brought to the cowstalls. Summer was easier as the cattle grazed on the grass fields which had well kept hedges and fences.

By 1948 milking was no longer done by hand in most farms. There were milking machine buckets which had suction cup clusters to fit each udder, usually four in number. The milk was still taken to the farm dairy to be put in churns and cooled.

By 1960 dairy farmers were installing milking parlours with pipe lines to the bulk refrigerated storage tanks. The cows were collected for milking in an open yard and cowsheds were obsolete. Larger sheds were put up for feeding with long troughs and hay racks. While one man was milking another would be filling the troughs with food and the racks with hay. When milking was over the animals would feed themselves. This reduced labour yet again. The milk was now collected by a bulk tanker to be taken to the dairies for bottling.

By the late 1970s faming in Studham was changing. Most farmers no longer kept cows and beef animals were in favour. Cereal crops were grown as they were more profitable. Tractors and all implements had got larger and more work could be done by fewer workers.

During the 1980s as farms became arable the cattle disappeared. Today out of the original seven farms in Studham only one has a herd of beef cattle and none have any milking herds.'

FLOWERS AND VEGETABLES

'My father-in-law Frederick Rook, aged 94½ years, relates this memory of the 1900s, when Broom was well known for miles around as the village that supplied the famous Crosse & Blackwell Co, London, also Sheldrakes, London, with onions, gherkins and cauliflowers for their pickling business. Mr John King of Manor Farm (whose son Jack was later to purchase Broom Hall) was the farmer who grew these vegetables, in fact he farmed most of the ground around Broom, over 1,000 acres.

Men with horses tilled the land, while other men hoed. At harvest time, the onions were first horse-hoed with one blade, then were pulled and laid in rows to dry. This was done by men, local women and schoolchildren in their summer holidays. The onions were then loaded into carts, brought back to Manor Farm where women from Biggleswade, Stanford, Clifton, Southill, Shefford, Langford (all walked, no bicycles) and Broom, peeled them. There were four hovels with a long corridor going right through all the hovels, and they had forms to sit on. The women collected the onions from the yard, then carried them inside in big round tins (which had previously been used for jam). They loaded the trays with onions, balanced on their knees, and peeled away, putting the peeled onions in small barrels filled with water. They were a jolly crowd, much joking, laughter and telling "tall" stories. At 4pm a bell was rung and the women formed a queue when the weighing commenced. The measure was made of wood (hooped round) with handles, when it overflowed it weighed a peck and a pint. For each peck and pint brass tokens were given, these were collected and come Friday at 4pm the women queued at Broom Farm House to be paid according to their tokens collected. The men would clear the onion peelings from the hovels, to be clean and ready for the women onion peeling the next day.

One man was employed all year, in charge of making brine and topping up the barrels of onions, which were then sealed with barrel top and "bung". The onions were graded into sizes; when sealed, the barrels were put on two rows of sleepers (edgeway down) for storing. The onion barrels when sent to London (they were drained first) were loaded onto a trolley the size of a small lorry, and pulled by two horses to Biggleswade station to be sent by train to King's Cross, then onto Crosse & Blackwell in London. The cauliflowers were cut into small florets, and these and the gherkins, to which nothing was done, were packed and sent also by train to the pickle factory.

Fred's father was foreman and when harvesting and peeling was over, he went back to his workshop. He was also the cooper, and he repaired and made new barrels for the next season. A small market was held on Broom Green on Friday afternoons, selling china, saucepans and various household items. Catching the ladies after being paid!

This industry finished during the First World War. Fred remembers many stories of this time, and recalls one old chap saying "I never worry if I've got tuppence more than I can spend"!'

'Until the Second World War there was no professional person living in Roxton, everybody worked on the land and besides farms there were 20 market gardeners sending high class vegetables to the London markets. This village was one of the first to grow brussels sprouts from about 1912 onwards, and contributed to better wages and more prosperity for the younger workers in agriculture.'

'In wintertime in the late 1930s gangs of pickers descended on North Bedfordshire for the "sproutin'", "toppin'", or as some would say, "been in the greens all winter". I have seen 40 pickers in one field. There were lorries from Bedford, B.H. King at Sandy, Coopers Aves at Bywaters, Wagers from St Neots, and from some large farmers who had their own, all taking tons of sprouts to Spitalfields, Brentford and Covent Garden, to big cities in the North and up to Manchester. Often a driver would do two trips a night to a London market to do a round of drops, then bring back empty boxes and bags. As we walked to school we would see bags of sprouts and tops carried out of the roadside fields by the pickers, four bags at a time. When lunchtime came round they rarely sat down, often pacing up and down to keep warm, eating their "Bavour" and drinking from a flask of tea.'

'During the 1930s I lived in Caldecote, near Biggleswade,

where my father was a very hard working market gardener. Our holidays were always last minute surprises, which added to our excitement. My father would come in during the day and say to my mother "I think we could go on holiday tomorrow for a few days". Either the weather was cold, so the crops of vegetables, and in later years, the flowers, were not coming on as fast as expected, or else it had been very hot and there had been a glut, followed by a lull. How my mother prepared and packed our clothes in such a short time, I do not know as I had three sisters with three and a half years between each of us.

We had three shire horses, which my eldest sister and I loved to ride. We would meet the horsekeeper as he came back from the fields and he would lift us up, my sister behind me, holding on to me tightly. The horses were very wide, so our feet stuck straight out sideways. One day the horsekeeper forgot to lift us off, before taking the horse into the stable. My feet caught the door posts, and we both promptly slid down the horse's tail. Fortunately the horse was our very gentle white horse, Bonny, and he stood perfectly still. We were only bruised but my father was furious with the horsekeeper and we did not get another ride for a long time.

We moved from our rented house in the fields when I was ten years old. My father had had a house built on a piece of his own land. He had a large tank for irrigation so we could then grow flowers. It made no difference how many flowers we had, no one worked on Sundays. If the irrigation had to be attended to, my father would see to it himself on Saturday evening. The only person who came in on a Sunday was the horsekeeper to feed the horses.

Life really took some arranging to be able to go out for the day on a Bank Holiday Monday. Although we had a "gang" of ladies who normally cut the flowers, my father never expected them to work on a holiday because of their families. The men would come early to cut and bunch the flowers and put them in water. Then my father, my eldest sister and I would pack the flowers into boxes and label them, ready for them to be collected for Covent Garden Market. We learnt to do this work when we were very young. When all this was done, we would be ready to go, perhaps to the seaside for the day, by 10am.'

LIFE IN SERVICE

The girls too, had few choices when they left school. Domestic service was often the only chance to earn a living, and if they found a good master or mistress it was at least a secure life, and provided many a tale to tell of Them and Us!

LACK OF CHOICE

'I suppose when I was young life was very basic compared to today. To begin with there was very little money about and wages were hardly adequate to feed and clothe a family. We were always well fed and clothed, my mother being such a wonderful manager. She made jams, marmalade, cakes, just everything, and lots of our clothes too. We were lucky to have a big garden to grow all our own vegetables, also keep poultry and have lovely fresh eggs.

There was no fitted carpet just a sort of coconut matting, very rough to the knees I remember, and bare bricks in the kitchen. The cooking stove which was heated by coal or wood had to be cleaned daily with black lead which looked lovely when it was done.

Most men earned their living by working on the farms but after the First World War there was no work to be had and when my father was demobbed the four of us had to live on 14 shillings a week; life was very difficult for parents then. Country children did not have the opportunity to choose a career like they can today, most boys followed in their father's footsteps if he had a trade or worked in agriculture and the girls helped in the home or went into service which meant living away from home. I would have liked to be a nurse but living ten miles from the nearest town there would have been money to find for board and lodging and also for a uniform. All this was out of the question so I went into service until the Second World War.'

'Not many married women worked outside the home, though a few took in washing. Home making was a full time job, added to the lack of opportunity and travelling facilities. Girls leaving school mostly had to go away into domestic service, living at the place of work and cycling home on their half day off and maybe every other Sunday afternoon. A few girls managed to get work in shops, but this entailed a cycle ride and perhaps a train journey night and morning and shop pay was very poor.'

MAIDS OF ALL WORK

'My mother had a maid, Nellie. She had left school at twelve to go into service. She was offered £10 a year. Mother's friends all said it was too much as you could get a girl from the orphanage for £5. She was provided with morning and afternoon uniforms but never had to wear a cap. She was given a room of her own – a change from her home where four of them shared a double bed – two top and two bottom.

She started to court the village policeman who was allowed into the kitchen once a week for an hour but they had to sit on opposite sides of the table. Nellie married her policeman and he went on to become a superintendent.'

'I left school at 13 and was put out to service. I went to Mount Pleasant at Stagsden. I was allowed to visit home on a Sunday afternoon for tea, walking home and back at night. I earned two shillings and sixpence per week. My parents would always walk me back in the dark evenings. Food was provided also a print dress for mornings, and black dress with aprons for afternoons and evenings. I used to eat in the same room as the family, but always at a small separate table, never at the same table as the family. In the evenings I had to clean the silver, and I remember I had a small bedroom of my own.

In later years my father purchased an old bike for me to ride home at weekends. I was there two years. I left to go to a rectory at Carlton looking after the small children, again I would cycle home on a Sunday for tea. Again I spent two years. Then war came.

In 1917 I made munitions at W H Allen until the end of the war. This time I lived in "digs" in Honey Hill Road (and we had two girls in a bed); the people of Queens Park all took in lodgers during this period of the war and prospered well. Here I met my future husband at the factory.

After the war I went back to service in Kimbolton Road and again lived in. Then I was married at 20.

We rented a house in Albert Street. Later we moved to Dudley Street so we could have two brothers for lodgers, and I would do office cleaning at night at Davies the coal merchant. The rent was £1 per week (1928–1935). I joined a building society, and eventually this enabled us to buy our own house in 1936.'

'When I was in my teens, I went to work as a parlour maid at our local vicarage. It was a very large house with many bedrooms, a drawing room, dining room and the vicar's study where he spent a lot of time.

The vicar and his wife were a very old couple, but very nice kind people. Although I think the vicar's appearance was sometimes made fun of, as he had a long white beard, and stuttered when agitated.

Elsie, my friend, was the cook and she looked after the kitchen and scullery, while I was busy with bedrooms and the downstairs. Also I waited at table for meals, and afternoon tea was served in the drawing room. Always at four o'clock I had to prepare a tray, and take it to the drawing room. My mistress would then serve the tea herself.

171

One winter afternoon, the mistress was out and I prepared tea for the vicar. I took in the three-tiered cakestand and a plate of bread and butter. With both hands full, I realised I had not put out the small table by the fire. As the vicar was not in the room, I just put the plate of bread and butter on his chair for a moment. Then I turned round to pick up the table to place it near his chair, only to find he had quietly walked into the room and, to my dismay, had sat down on the bread and butter in his chair.

What to do? I just said "Oh dear, sir, I am afraid you are sitting on the bread and butter." He jumped up saying "What! What! What!" and turned to look. I quickly picked two slices from his bottom and put them back onto the plate, then quickly disappeared to the kitchen, where I am afraid laughter overcame me.'

'At one time clothes were very distinctive of class. There was the maidservant who on her half day off wore her best hat with a flower on it. Her mistress said to her: "What, your best hat, you will ask for an egg for your breakfast next!"

The Bishop came to dinner one night after service at the home of the rector. Much preparation was made for the gravity of the meal but when the maid proudly bore the leg of mutton into the dining room she stumbled and shot the meat under the table. The Bishop rose to the moment and helped her up, remarking "The first time I have been chased by a sheep".

OTHER WAYS WE MADE A LIVING

For those who continued to live at home, rather than going into service there were the cottage industries of straw plaiting for the hatting industry and lace making, and a small living to be made from the countryside, picking wild fruits and flowers for sale.

For the men who did not earn their living from the land, there was employment to be had at the brickworks and trades such as carpentry and work on the railways.

PLAIT AND HATS

'Although the National school and British schools respectively were springing up in Luton from 1835, schooling was not then compulsory and Lucy did not go to school early in life. As a small child she earned money from making straw plait, as did many young children at their Mother's knee. This money was used to enable them to learn the use of the new machines in the hat factory and the money earned from this in turn was spent to educate Lucy at an evening school for girls. This exceptional woman went on to marry and have eleven surviving children and with the help of one servant girl and an older daughter ran a large household and virtually ran her husband's hat factory as well. At a time of acute poverty she was Mother to the neighbourhood – everyone ran to her for help on every matter imaginable – if she was

173

unable to do it herself, she directed the broken bones to the doctor.

This was Doris Rickard's mother and one can imagine what a fortunate child Doris was to be the youngest but one of eleven in this caring family. Her father and mother owned a hat factory at a time when the hat trade was the major industry in Luton. Later in his career Doris's father gave up the factory and made panama hats for the men in the Royal Family for Henry Heath's famous London firm.

The Rickards were in 'comfortable circumstances' and with such a large family quantities of food were prepared as they kept open house for friends. Doris's mother, along with other families at the time, always looked to help those who were poorer and in need. Food from the table was sent to those in need of it together with outgrown shoes and clothes. All this benevolence was extended without patronising the poorer folk. Luton was then a small community – everyone knew everyone else and it was accepted that they helped each other. It was a time of acute poverty with no welfare system and only the Assistance Board to turn to. In these instances the Relieving Officer (Doris's father-in-law at one time) went round to the homes of the poor, who were made to sell everything but the barest necessities before a few shillings were handed out.

It was the people in more comfortable positions financially who helped the poor. And the people willingly helped all they could.'

'Luton was a unique town and a fortunate town in many ways, the first being that because of the quality of the wheat grown in Bedfordshire the hat industry came into being. Children made the plait for the straw hats at their mother's knee in order to bring in extra money to supplement the very low wages of the agricultural workers at the time. As hat manufacturing grew to become the major industry in Luton, the outworkers grew in numbers and a major part of the industry was carried out in people's homes. Horses and traps picked up and distributed work around the town, but women also walked to Luton with their work carried in black bags from outlying villages such as Caddington and Slip End from which areas there was no public transport. A large percentage of women continued to work on hats throughout their lives – thus Luton was one of the few areas where married women continued to work after marriage and children, laying the foundation of what was to become the norm 70 years or so later.

The hat trade brought jobs for women at a time when there were few options – domestic service being the largest employer until the factories and offices came into being. Further education and training for the professions ie nursing and teaching – were for the privileged few.'

'After leaving school at Tingrith most girls in the 1920s went into service at the manor house or the rectory. Some were lucky to get a shop job or hat work in Luton. The problem regarding the latter jobs was getting to Harlington station to catch a train to Luton as you had to walk some four miles there and back again in the pitch dark, with no street lighting. One of my sisters worked at Woburn Hospital when it was run by the Duchess of Bedford; she was allowed one half day off a fortnight to visit her family.'

LACE AT THE COTTAGE DOOR

'Women at Stevington in the early years of the century did the housework and lacemaking. When hot in the summer, they used to sit outside their front doors with their pillows. The lace was always sold to Braggins and Sowmans who came from Olney with his travelling shop.'

FROM RAILWAYS TO PRIMROSES

'Between the wars many of the Stevington men worked at J.P. White's, high class woodwork and french polishing. They did work for many prestigious buildings and one man helped to make the present that Bedfordshire gave to the then Princess Elizabeth when she got married. Others worked at the Swan Model Laundry at Bromham, at Allens the engineers in Bedford, and on the railways. Nearly everyone cycled to work, often in groups of four or six.

An unpleasant duty for railway workers would occur in bad weather, when they might be called out of their beds in the night to go "fogging" with lamps on foggy nights or to keep the water tanks at Oakley free of ice in frosty weather.'

'Dad worked in Bedford and walked there and back daily, about five miles each way, leaving at about six o'clock after having a cup of tea and slice of bread. He always had a cooked breakfast on Sunday mornings – cooked with the fat cut off the cured pig hanging up.'

'The brickworks between Green End and West End at

176

Kempston at the beginning of the century were run by three old men. They would dig the clay and mould the bricks in boxes like shoe boxes and then push them into the fire. They didn't like to be watched and we children would be chased away if they saw us.'

'My father cycled to the London Brick Company to work. He did shift work, one week days and one week nights, and it was very difficult for my mother keeping four of us occupied and quiet when he slept during the day.'

'If the men were ill and no money came in, then the women would take in extra washing to earn a few shillings to feed their family. In the late summer we would pick the blackberries from the hedgerows and put them in a large basket, and they would be sold on a Saturday at Houghton Regis and Dunstable. I did not go out to work as I stayed at home to help on the field; my father used to take the vegetables, eggs and rabbits on a round, using a horse-drawn trolley both before and after the war.'

'In the summer months at Tempsford between the wars, from June onwards, the women would set off with their buckets and stools, often being taken by lorry to go pea picking in nearby fields.'

'The elderly Miss Measures, Miss Alice and Miss Gertie, lived at Bletsoe Cottage. In those days, wild flowers grew in profusion and Miss Alice went to Pippin Wood to pick primroses in the spring. She bunched them and took them to Bedford to sell.'

GETTING ABOUT

The age of horse transport is not far behind us, and for many people 'getting about' quite simply meant walking! The bicycle brought a new freedom between the wars, but it was the country buses which opened up new horizons for villagers.

CHANGING TIMES

'One of my mother's earliest memories, in the early 1900s, was going to the Meet at Bromham Swan in the governess cart because they had heard someone was coming from Newport Pagnell in a motor car!'

'Early in the century, apart from trains and pony and trap, travel by the ordinary villager was by foot. Our hallowed footpaths of today were often tracks where people walked across the fields, either to work or the quickest way to perhaps visit relatives in a neighbouring village. Then as bicycles became more accessible the footpaths fell into disuse and with the great food effort during the war were ploughed up and lost. Only in this last decade have footpaths been resurrected to be used purely for the pleasure of walking.

The village carrier was the man who was the villagers' chief contact with the outside world. He fetched and carried anything for people that couldn't be carried by themselves. He went to town on market days and brought back for people things needed which couldn't be acquired in the village. Often folk who had need to go to town themselves rode with the carrier.

At Carlton one such carrier was Mr Franklin, whose business was later taken over by his daughter Eva and her husband Albert. Their first motorized lorry or van was open at the back and seemed very high from the ground so it had a little ladder as access to the back; this novelty gave the boys of the village an opportunity to steal a ride sitting on the steps at the back. Road safety wasn't a matter of concern. However Eva decided to ride in the back herself to reprimand the naughty boys. Well into the late 1930s if in Bedford on a Saturday or Wellingborough on Wednesdays, Eva could be spotted cutting about doing shopping for others. Theirs was the first daily bus service into Bedford, operated by their nephew Geoff, who coped with this new enterprise, not always on time, but became a noted and liked character en route. So from these beginnings people began to move around to see the outside world for themselves.'

'If shopping in Bedford, five miles away, in the early years of the century, we travelled in the horse and cart, a great delight, but to do this we had to book several weeks in advance, and the horse and cart only ran on Saturdays. The cost was sixpence return and threepence for children. It left Stevington at ten o'clock and returned from Bedford at four o'clock. The coaching station was where Marks and Spencer in Midland Road is today, though in later years it moved to The Ship in St Cuthbert's. We never

179

stopped to eat anything during the day's shopping, but always waited until we were home.'

'An exciting excursion from Bletsoe between the wars was to go to Bedford on market day, that is on Wednesday or Saturday. At one time a carrier came through from Riseley and those who could afford it could go in to town by horse power. If you could afford a bike, you biked in, hoping you wouldn't have to dismount at Oakley Hill. Not everyone could afford a bike so they would set off early to walk the seven miles to Bedford. It was a different matter walking back. Later, the "Birch Bus" came along the A6 and picked up passengers at Bletsoe Turn.

During the 1940s mothers with babies thought nothing of walking to Sharnbrook to have the babies weighed and collect the orange juice or rosehip syrup. It used to be fun because all the mothers would meet with their prams and walk along together.'

BIKES, TRAMS AND BUSES

'In the 1930s my father cycled to work, and I can remember him having trouble at times with his carbide lamp. He would bring it indoors to repair and I can still recall the horrible smell of carbide.'

'Few people owned a car in the 1940s and most people used to cycle, or walk, to their destination. As teenagers at weekends we would cycle from Colesden to St Neots to do our shopping and leave our cycles in the now closed Fox and Hounds yard, then stand in a queue to go into the now demolished Pavilion Cinema, where a seat in the stalls was one shilling and ninepence. For a change we would cycle to Bedford. I well remember as a child we used to leave our cycles in Mr Savage's yard in Dame Alice Street; one could leave one's bike then and have no fear of it being stolen. Often we would cycle or bus, by Eastern National, to one of Bedford's four cinemas – the Granada had all the new releases and you paid two shillings and ninepence to sit upstairs. In the cricket season we would cycle to adjoining villages to fulfil a fixture, with bats or pads strapped to our cross bars.'

'In 1906 hansom cabs and horse-drawn buses came into being and in February 1908 trams were introduced to Luton. The trams ran from the depot in Park Street through George Street and out to Kingsway which would be on the edge of the town; out to Wardown Park along the New Bedford Road, and up to Round Green terminating at the Jolly Topers public house. But by 1932 the tramlines were being taken up to make way for the buses, so the time of tram travel was of short duration, a mere 24 years.

The trains first came to Luton in May 1858 when the first section of the railway was opened, the first journey being made to Dunstable. By 1860 there were trains every day to London King's Cross.

My memory of my early years is of walking everywhere. With my home being in Victoria Street (off Chapel Street) close to the town centre and relations in North Street (off Old Bedford Road), my life was encompassed in an area of two square miles.'

'If you wanted to go into Bedford from Stevington you would book your seat the previous Tuesday or Wednesday for Saturday morning, with Mr Stevens who had an old Bluebird bus with a canvas roof, which was opened in summer. The bus was kept down at the Manor and on Saturday mornings Mr Stevens would drive us into Bedford and park the bus in a yard behind The Ship in Mill Street.'

'A green double decker bus travelled between the villages around Wootton and Bedford during the 1930s. Sometimes Dad would take one of us to Bedford for shopping on a Saturday. I can still recall the "bacony" smell of Sainsbury's, and remember how we used to love to watch the butter being patted into shape so quickly and expertly.'

'Between the wars at Dean, people gradually obtained bicycles and would ride five miles to Kimbolton, eight miles to Rushden and for the first time found employment outside the village. In the 1930s Mr Woodham's carrier bus ran a service to Bedford each Saturday at two shillings and sixpence return. Then the United Counties began a Wednesday and Saturday service to Bedford. Eventually a daily bus ran and girls got domestic work in Bedford. Some bought bicycles to ride home 15 miles on their half days off.'

'Transport for Salford in between the wars was one bus to Bedford and back on Saturdays. To get a train people had to walk or cycle to Ridgemont or Woburn Sands stations.

It was not until after the war had started and the evacuees came that a bus service operated through the village twice daily in between Bedford and Bletchley. Sadly the service ceased several years ago and for a time the only bus was on a Tuesday to Woburn Sands and back to enable people to visit the post office. Now we have this service on Friday also and a Community Bus to Bedford every Wednesday giving roughly two hours shopping. Saturdays a bus runs through the village to Milton Keynes leaving at 10.20am and returning at 2.50pm. At no time has any transport ever been useful for going to and from work.'

WAR & PEACE

THE GREAT WAR

Though the front line fighting may have been far away, those left at home in Bedfordshire had to face the dangers and tragedies of war from 1914 to 1918, seeing the young men of their town or village march off to fight and being able to welcome so few back home again. There were shortages too, and the Zeppelins.

VILLAGE LIFE THROUGH THE WAR

'My earliest memories of home were of the village of Tebworth during the First World War, a small insignificant village between Toddington and the Watling Street. My mother moved there with myself, a baby, and my brother Leslie who was about six or seven years old. My father, after training as a Gunner in the Beds and Herts Regiment, stationed at Biscot Camp in Luton, had gone off "to the war" – France – and my mother moved from Luton to the village where she was born and brought up, to be near her parents. Sarah and Alfred Hack were well known in the village and lived on a small farm – Buttercup Farm was its "posh" name, but I don't think it was used much. It was in the middle of the village by the village green, with large black barn, a cobbled yard, various buildings (pig-sties etc) and two fields behind. My grandfather, as well as keeping pigs and hens (and sometimes sheep), was agent for

186

Mr Lockhart of Dunstable (coal merchant) and supplied coal in hundredweights and half hundredweights to most people in the village. He delivered it by wheelbarrow. My grandmother did a small bit of trading from the same source, namely a large block of salt which she cut up to sell – a penny or twopence a time. The loose salt was her "perks"; the 13th piece was her profit! I used to be allowed to play with the loose salt on a newspaper and loved its lovely white crunchy texture. But her main work in the village was the local midwife, and she was called out to all births and looked after the mother and baby for a week or so afterwards. She was also layer-out of the dead, which she did with kindness and skill. "Mis 'Ack" as she was known, was loved by all her "babies", in fact by everyone. She and Grandad were faithful members of the Methodist chapel.

Mum, Leslie and I lived next door to the pub – the Queen's Head, and outside our home was the village pump. I used to look out of the window to see the men collect the day's water and I always looked for my Uncle Sid who came with two buckets suspended from a yoke. He had quite a way to carry his water – drinking water that is; most people had a well or water butt for soft water for washing etc. Uncle Sid and his brother Fred owned the Timber Yard which employed most of the men of the village who were not farm workers. Most of the women I think cycled into Dunstable to work at Waterlow's the printers. My mother used to tell a tale about the time Waterlow's first opened. She then as a girl lived at Crab Terrace on the Wingfield Road, and when the sound of Waterlow's hooter boomed out across the fields people were terrified – they thought it was the "last trump" and ran out in fear not knowing what it was. This only happened if the wind was blowing in the right direction!

My brother being four years older than me went to school and when the bell rang I cried to go as well. The school mistress was very kind and allowed me to go when I was about three and a half years old, but I guess she was sorry! The first day I was given a tray of sand and a stick to make letters in the sand. "Oh lovely stuff," I thought it was brown sugar and began to eat it! Finding out my mistake I threw the lot on the floor and my poor brother was sent for from the "big room" to sweep it up. But I wasn't punished or banned from the school; I learned to read and write, before we went back to Luton in 1919–1920, but as I was not yet five years old I could not go to school until after my birthday. Living in the country we were lucky to have vegetables, milk, eggs etc but my mother used to cycle to Leighton Buzzard to try to get "unrationed" food for us. There were three small shops in the village; the post office, which we could see from our window, and knew when the grocer's van called and we might get sweets. Then Polly Pratt's, where we also (sometimes) got sweets and Alice Day who had a shop in her front room "down the lane" where her daughter Win always sat at the door to call her mother when there was a customer.

As I said, we lived next to the pub; and the people who kept it were Londoners, named Nunn. Their son Billy was my age and we were friends. On summer Saturdays and Sundays charabancs full of noisy visitors would come to the pub and always threw out pennies and halfpennies for us when they went off home. I got hit in the eye once! Another accident I had was when I got up from the rug in front of the fire as my mother was filling the tea pot. I got boiling tea all over my head and my poor mother, in a panic, put spirits of camphor on it instead of camphorated oil! I "lived to tell the tale". Two more episodes worthy of mention come to my mind. One night we had news of a Zeppelin approaching our area, and we children were taken from our beds, wrapped in blankets, and carried off "down the lane" to escape any bombs or whatever else might happen. I don't think anything did! I suppose when it was daylight we all trailed back again. When my father eventually came home I was as usual "over at Grandma's" and someone was sent to fetch me home. Not having seen this strange man (and not wanting to be torn away from my play, I expect), I was dragged screaming across the village, saying "I don't *want* to see my Daddy!" but afterwards of course I wouldn't leave him and became his little shadow. He was one of the fortunate ones and did not suffer any war-wounds; that is until he got off the train at Dunstable at the end of the journey and had the train door smash the fingers of one hand!'

BEGINNING TO END

'One morning when we were nearly at Cople school at the start of the First World War, we heard someone blowing a bugle so we went past the school to see what it was about. When we got to the church corner we saw it was a fellow named Charlie Brunt, blowing the bugle to call all the young men of the village to go and enlist in the army. I remember being in the playground when one of the chaps came home and he said they all passed except one man, who was very cross-eyed.

189

During the war there were hundreds of soldiers under canvas in one of the fields on Oak Farm with their mules and horses. The mules were tethered in rows in the middle of the field and there were four rows of horse chestnut and lime trees down one side of the field. They stretched beyond Oak Farm and were the old squire's carriage way years ago. The soldiers had thick ropes round the trees all the way down the avenue, as the field is still called, where they tied their horses and you can still see the marks where the ropes cut into the trees. We have ploughed the field for ever so many years now but you can still find some old mule shoes. Once when I was ploughing the headland I went a bit nearer the spinney and I heard something rattle and when I looked round I saw I had ploughed out scores of old mule and horse shoes. You could always tell a mule's shoe from a horse's shoe because they were long and not so round. The old mules used to break loose at night and go roaming round the farm but they would be back in the morning when they heard the bugle blow for feeding time.

I well remember we were ploughing down against the High Road when a man came puffing up the hill pushing his bike and he was so excited as he shouted out "The war's over, mate!" That was on 11th November 1918. The man I was driving plough for said "Cards up guv'nor" and he jumped on his bike and went down the pub to celebrate, leaving me to take the three horses home myself.'

'I was only two years old at the beginning of the war but I just remember my two uncles, my mother's brothers, joining up. I was carried on their shoulders across the fields from Shelton Road to The Three Compasses inn to join their army regiment. I think it was 1915. In 1916 they were both killed in France.'

'When I was quite young I was staying with my grand-parents in March, Cambridgeshire, and my grandmother sent me into the small town centre to a friend who had a photographer's shop, to get a photograph taken to be sent away to my father who was in the trenches in France. Grandma thought it would be nice to have one taken in my nightdress with candlestick and teddy bear – so off I went on my own. There were no cars and very little traffic so it was quite safe for me to go on my own. However, as I passed the local butcher's shop my arch enemy, the butcher's daughter, ran out and made rude remarks about my beloved teddy bear Edward. I gave her a punch on the nose and we had such a fight, that I arrived at the photographer's with a black eye and my hair ribbon in shreds – so I had to go a week later instead.

During the First World War, I lived for a time with my Aunt Gertrude in Ramsey (Hunts) and my mother had a job at the local undertaker's workshop where wooden cases were made for containing shells. She and her friend were "Inspectors" and they had to make sure that there were no projecting nails. The workshop was bitterly cold, so Mother and her friend always ate their lunch in the hearse, and they thought that they were probably the only people lunching in a hearse when peace was declared.'

'My grandmother entertained troops during the war – the Welsh who were great singers and took a piano out on a haywain to the fields, and the Highlanders who could also sing but spoke mostly Gaelic. They suffered an epidemic of measles and died like flies and are buried in Kempston cemetery. The Australians the family got to know always came back to them for leave.'

'The First World War is remembered by some WI members in Dunstable. Memories include sheltering from Zeppelins in the cellar, and seeing one passing over the town.'

'In 1915 my father joined the Beds and Herts Regiment and trained at Ampthill Park. His name appears on the war memorial in Wymington and on the Roll of Honour in Edinburgh Castle; he was transferred to the Royal Scots Regiment. He was reported missing in 1916, after he had been home in his kilt and gaiters. We later were informed he had died of wounds in Germany. In 1919 all of his effects were returned to my mother. She received a widow's pension of just 52 shillings and two pence to keep herself and three children. My mother died at the age of 36 years. I then went to live with an aunt in Thrapston.'

THE SECOND WORLD WAR

When war came again to Bedfordshire, it brought, amongst other things, the American airmen who flew missions from newly built airfields all over the county.

Tales of their generosity soon spread and the children, and the girls, loved these glamorous strangers! More prosaically, but just as vital to the war effort, men who were in reserved occupations or too young or too old for the forces, did their bit in the Local Defence Volunteers, soon to be known as the Home Guard.

SOLDIERS AND AIRMEN

'War came and the tanks and lorries drove regularly past our house at Bromham. We children waved and shouted with excitement and were often thrown handfuls of sugar and sweets by the soldiers. Mum and her neighbours provided pots of tea and cakes on the front lawn when the convoys stopped for a rest. Dad was in the Home Guard and often went on duty after a long day in the brickfield.'

'In 1941 Tempsford airfield was opened and the RAF arrived, although it wasn't known at the time that many famous members of the Resistance came and went from Tempsford to be dropped secretly over France.'

'Wartime in Little Staughton was quite exciting for us children, it opened up a whole new world. There were searchlights and anti-aircraft units nearby and Lancaster bombers and Mosquitoes operating from our airfield, and Flying Fortresses were also based locally. We met many foreigners but how I regret not learning to speak Italian and German from the prisoners of war who lived and worked on our farm.

To help entertain the servicemen and women, whist

drives were organised and villagers donated rations to provide refreshments. The American airforcemen gave the children of the village a party at Christmas which was a great treat. The village school was well attended, even more so when evacuees were billeted in the village during the war.'

'Parts of Thurleigh airfield lie in the parish of Bletsoe and there was great excitement when in September 1942, the first American airmen came over. There were 1,700 of them and they belonged to the 306th Bomb Group, USAAF. There were four squadrons of Boeing B-17s, Flying Fortresses: the 367th, known as The Eager Beavers; the 368th, The Clay Pigeons; the 369th, Fightin' Bitin'; and the 423rd, The Grim Reapers. By the end of hostilities, they had flown 9,614 sorties; 171 bombers based on the airfield were lost.

David recalls playing on the edge of the airfield and watching for the squadrons to come home. As they approached the runway the children looked out for the flares that the aircraft sent up prior to landing. A green flare meant that all personnel had returned safely; an orange and green flare meant they had injured men on board but a red flare meant that yet another of the airmen had died during the sortie.

Edie recalls that when she was working on her brother-in-law's farm very near the runway, the pilots would deliberately come in to land very low so as to see them fall flat to the ground. One bomber was so low that it removed the outhouse roof where the bucket lavatory was.

Contrary to what people said, the airmen were not

194

always well off. They would sell nylons and candy to people in Bletsoe who could afford to buy, and spend the extra money down at the Falcon Inn.

Not surprisingly, the airmen were always on the look-out for pretty girls. There were plenty of secluded country walks and they were well used. Mr Smith at Coplar Farm noticed the interest these couples had in his haystacks. He put a notice on his farm gate:

If you find my haystack handy
I've got kids and they like candy . . .

Bags of sweets and chocolate bars were regularly left by the haystacks after that.

All the bombs for the American Air Force base at Thurleigh came by train to Sharnbrook station. There they were loaded onto lorries and they were stored in Bourne End Lane until they were wanted and then they were taken up to the base. Nobody could use Bourne End Lane unless they had a special pass; it was all barricaded with barbed wire.'

THE HOME GUARD

'During the war we used to belong to the Home Guard. We had to go training at nights and Sunday mornings, then we had to be out all one night guarding bridges or railway stations. I have been out all night many a time and gone home about six in the morning. I'd go straight down the meadow to fetch the horses, almost too tired to walk, but after a bit of breakfast you were out in the fields again, working all day.

Mr Vincent, who owned the farm where I worked at Cople, joined the Home Guard and finished up as Colonel. Jim Turnbull and I were in his platoon at Northill and we both ended up as Sergeants. One night when Jim was in charge at Blunham station he thought he had lost a round out of his sten gun so early in the morning they spent about an hour looking for it. They couldn't find it so they went home. On the next night we went on parade and I remember we were sitting under a big chestnut tree. When Jim sat down he banged the gun on the ground between his knees and it went off, just missing his nose. The bullet had been in the gun all the time.

One weekend we went to camp at Sutton under canvas. The ground was very sandy there and I remember seeing Major Barry outside his tent with his face lathered ready for a shave, when suddenly my young brother went by at speed in a truck and shot sand all over his face. He wasn't very pleased, but I don't think he ever found out who'd done it.

I had just been ill for six weeks with the mumps so I wasn't feeling too good and one of the officer's servants came into our tent early in the morning with half a bottle of whisky from the officers mess. He said to me "Have some of this, it'll make you feel better", so I drank as much of it as I could, then went for a walk in the woods. I remember I hadn't got far when I saw a tree trunk across the path and I couldn't get over it so I sat down against it and went to sleep for two or three hours. When I woke up I felt a lot better. Then in the afternoon we were inspected by the Queen on Biggleswade football ground. We had to march past the Queen with fixed bayonets with the Beds and Herts band playing, then we marched up Biggleswade and someone gave the order to march at ease. The bayonets were flying all over the place and I can remember Colonel Vincent shouting "Who the hell gave that order?" I thought it was a bit dangerous!'

AIR RAIDS REMEMBERED

'Up the wooden hill to Bedfordshire!

How many generations of children have been marched up the stairs with these words in their ears?

Certainly as a small child growing up in London during the war I had heard it many times, and often wondered about that mysterious place.

In 1941 night time raids became so frequent that our trips "up the hill" were stopped and Father obtained a Morrison shelter – basically a large metal table – and had it erected in the sitting room so that the family could sleep safely downstairs.

As a five year old who was frightened of the dark, I loved the feeling of security when we were all, Mother, Father, nine year old sister and two year old brother, tucked up together – Grandfather slept under the dining room table.

Then one night that security was shattered! All the family were asleep when a knock came at the door, the Air Raid Warden had come to tell us that a time-bomb had been dropped up the road, and as we and our home were in danger, we must leave and go to the community shelter in the park. I remember my mother taking charge of the situation, telling my father to go ahead with Grandfather as he could not walk so fast, and dressing us in our warmest clothes.

Soon we were ready to go, gas masks across our chests, my brother in his pram and on our way into the noisy night. Aeroplanes were droning overhead, guns sounded and searchlights probed the sky, as very frightened we hurried to meet the others – or so we thought!

As we came to the shelter and were about to descend the long slope into the ground, a man appeared at the door. His face is still very clear to me after all this time. "Sorry," he shouted, "there's no room in here!" I can still hear the panic in my mother's voice, up to then she had been quite calm, organising us all, but this was the last straw. "You must let us in, I'm looking for my husband and father-in-law." But no amount of talking would persuade him even to look for the rest of the family, and certainly not to let us in. Once more we were sent out into the night not knowing where to go, Mother talking to calm us down.

Suddenly a voice from the dark interrupted us. "Is that children's voices I can hear?" Coming across the road was a man we knew slightly, an Air Raid Warden who lived nearby. There was no mistaking my mother's relief in sharing her problem with somebody else, and his indignation that anyone should let children wander the streets in such terrible conditions. There was no point in moving on, he told us, as everywhere else was full up, but we could go with him back to his house.

At last we were inside, away from the noise of battle, all of us tucked up in one large bed. As I lay there trying to sleep I turned over in my mind, what I would later recognize as the irony of the situation. We had been turned out of our home and our new "safe" shelter, had walked through the night with guns and bombs around us and were now lying *upstairs* quite likely to be destroyed at any time. At this point I must have slept, but I'm sure my mother lay there worrying about her home and family and wondering if we would come out alive.

Happily for us the day dawned with no more interruptions, and soon we all met up again at home which had only lost a few windows. It would be sometime before we would be going "up the wooden hill" again, and nearly 30 years before I would settle and become acquainted with Bedfordshire.'

STRANGERS IN OUR MIDST

Even before war was declared, evacuees began to arrive in Bedfordshire – some to stay and some to return to London as fast as they possibly could, bombs or no bombs! There were other strangers too, Italian and German prisoners of war, who worked on the land alongside local men and women.

THE EVACUEES ARRIVE

'When war broke out many children were evacuated to Bedfordshire and lived in the villages. There was fun and pathos, school space was limited, and one dinner lady produced 80 hot dinners in a tiny kitchen in a church room. The Londoners were not used to dark streets and longed for the fish and chip shops, cinemas and pubs. But many firm friendships were forged, both with children and teaching staff.'

'It was Friday, 1st September 1939, and the day I first came face to face with sadness and bewilderment.

I shall never forget the sight of children, younger than my eleven years, arriving in Luton as evacuees from London. They looked so confused and lost as they clutched their small cases or carrier bags, with their gas masks slung from their shoulders.

Three of these children, sisters ranging down from eight years old, were billeted on my grandmother.

Then on that fateful sunny Sunday morning, 3rd September, I listened to the Prime Minister making the announcement that we were at war.

Grandma suggested I took the three little girls for a walk and during this walk, I gave, what I later realised, was a most misleading assurance.

The eldest evacuee was, naturally, very worried that her Daddy would have to go for a soldier. With the innocent wisdom of my eleven years, I assured her that he was much too old for that to happen.

I never had to face her when she would learn how wrong I was. Like so many other evacuees, the three sisters were taken back home by their mother during the phoney war.'

'We knew they were coming, but we didn't know when or from where and in the case of us children, we didn't know "what". "Vacooees" would definitely arrive – sometime.

They chose the end of the afternoon school playtime to appear. The whistle had blown and we were lined up, boys on the left, girls on the right, beautifully spaced by putting our hands on the shoulders of the child in front. The sun blazed down. The teachers disappeared, but, obedient six year olds that we were, we stood in line till our little arms ached and dropped to our sides. Gradually we realised that we were free. No adults had their beady eyes on us, because they were all doing urgent and important things with strange mothers and children, who were all climbing wearily out of a bus down the lane.

The next few days were very enlightening, as we learned from our new friends that milk came out of a tin and was called "condensed". The cows at the farm had nothing to do with its production, as we had previously believed. Fish and chips could be eaten hot or cold, at any hour of the day. Beds were for grown ups to sleep on and for children to sleep underneath. Above all, that the countryside was noisy. All those birds singing, cows mooing and sheep bleating, were more than the "vacooees'" mothers could bear. "We would rather face Hitler's bombs than live in this racket night and day" they said so off they went, back home to London and we returned to seating two at a desk at school, instead of three. The village was ours again.'

'I was six years old when the war started. At first, it didn't make much difference to us, but then my oldest brother went into the army and my father into the RAF, leaving my mother to look after myself and my brother and sister. Then came the blackout, and as my mother was a dressmaker she was able to make extra money making blinds for people in the village. She would sit at the old treadle sewing machine, her feet working like fury as the needle whizzed up and down the seams.

The only time we were allowed to go outside in the blackout was when we wanted to go to the lavatory, which was across the yard in a brick barn. Our lavatory was a galvanized bucket under a long closed-in bench with a hole in the top. We didn't think there was anything wrong with this as hardly anyone in our village had a proper toilet. My mother always made my sister take me across the yard, which made her very cross, especially if she was listening to ITMA or "Monday Night at Eight" on the wireless.

One day a WVS lady came to our front door holding the hand of a tearful little boy. His name was Eric from Bethnal Green, he was eight years old and our evacuee. Eric was not a very attractive child. He was skinny, dressed in rags and had a disfiguring harelip and a speech impediment caused by a cleft palate. My mother gave him a cuddle and a bath, dressed him in some of my brother's clothes and burnt his in the fire under the copper. That night she gave him some pyjamas to wear. He didn't know what to do with them so he put them over his jumper and trousers and got into bed. Eric proved to be a sweet natured little boy and idolized my mother who gave him a lot of love and always understood what he said when nobody else could. Was it coincidence or did the authorities know that she had had a baby with a cleft palate that had died at a few weeks old?

Eric had a brother called Ronnie who lived next door, a cheeky little cockney sparrow who was always getting into scrapes, and an older brother who lived with an old lady and was always running away. My mother reckoned we had the best of the bunch.

We didn't have many air raids, but when the siren went we children were made to sit under the large kitchen table. We thought it was great fun, except Eric, who was very frightened.

Sometimes we would see the convoys of tanks go by and the airmen from the nearby camp marching. My auntie had a wire haired terrier called Spot who loved to trot along behind the men. They made a great fuss of him and gave him titbits. No wonder he wanted to join the RAF.

One day Eric's father turned up and said that the bombing had eased off and as his wife missed the children he was taking them home. We were all sad to see him go and my mother was most upset.

We had other evacuees, Rosie and Donald who came from a better part of London and were plump and well cared for. My mother loved them, as she did all children but they could never take the place of Eric in her heart. We never heard from him again and I often wonder if he survived the war.'

'The first rumblings of the war came to Bletsoe with the advent of the evacuees. The children came from Walthamstow to Bedford station and then by bus to Bletsoe, a tiny village in North Bedfordshire with a population of only just over a hundred. Grace Bates, whose parents had a poultry farm in the village and whose brother still sells eggs today in Bletsoe, had the task of persuading the village people to take in one or two children. One pair of sisters had strict instructions that they had to be billeted together but, as is often the way with sisters, they didn't get on and seeing the opportunity of living in separate houses, each contrived to be placed with a friend and not with a sister. By persuasion and threat, Grace managed to get the whole allocation placed – no mean feat, for she was barely 20 – except for a family of five mixed race children, wild in the extreme. Every door closed to these children and Grace trailed back with them in tow. Fortunately, her parents took them in. However, sleepy Bletsoe ways were not to the taste of the Londoners and within six weeks they had returned to Walthamstow, preferring to risk the possibility of the Blitz to the dangers of country life.'

PRISONERS OF WAR

'We had a lot of Italian prisoners billeted in a large house on the next farm to the one I worked on at Cople. Some used to work with us and some were good workers while others didn't want to do anything if there were a few spots of rain. But we used to get on with them very well. Some of them were very clever and they used to make lovely baskets with willows and fruit baskets with straw. I remember I had a gold ring at the time and it kept dropping off my finger so one of them took a piece out of it and made it smaller and you couldn't see where it had been joined again.

I remember one young Italian who I used to work with a lot. He was always happy and singing. I said to him "They made you run at Alamein didn't they!". "I did run

204

very fast," he said, "Big victory no good to me when I am dead."'

'During and after the Second World War we were farming at Little Staughton and were asked to reclaim more land to grow vegetables and corn. It was very poor scrubland overgrown with brambles and blackthorn and as some of our employees had been called up we needed help from another source, therefore the prisoners of war came to help. We started off in 1942 with Italians who were billeted at a camp nearby, they came daily with a guard in attendance. When they had worked for us for a time we chose five promising workers and they were allowed to live away from the camp, in one of our bungalows looked after by an elderly lady. We thought the Italians were not very keen on hard work but every day an inspector came on his motorbike. They helped clear some of the land and also with the harvest which was not as mechanised as it is today. I did not cater for them but included in my weekly shopping were large strips of white fish which they ate raw.

These Italians stayed with us for about a year. We were then offered German prisoners; they were obviously used to hard work and knew what discipline meant. Six of the best workers camped in a large barn and one cooked but I did their shopping which presented language problems, particularly with rationing. We were mole draining the land, which meant digging deep trenches and filling them with rubble, hard but necessary work to drain very damp land. Our six prisoners always behaved very well knowing that we had the right to send them back to the camp if they did not. They were clever with their hands, producing rings and brooches from aluminium tins which they sold to local girls. They wanted dyes, possibly to dye their shirts, their jackets and trousers, which had a prison badge for easy and quick identification. They returned to the camp in 1945 and were repatriated. I believe they were quite happy to be here away from the fighting. Some married local or Land Army girls after the war and remained in England.'

THE LAND ARMY GIRLS

Many women from all over the country, and from all walks of life, joined the Women's Land Army as their war service. It was not an easy option, as they soon found out, but those who lasted the course discovered a love of farming and the countryside which never left them in later years.

'In 1940 I was living in Bangor, North Wales with my mother and sister who was only seven. We had moved there to get away from the nightly bombing in London, leaving my father behind to run his garage. After we had been in Wales a short while I received a letter saying I would have to do some war work and as I was training to be a shorthand typist I was asked to go to the Ministry of Food offices in Llandudno. I didn't want to leave my family so I joined the Land Army.

I duly reported to Lonisaf Farm, Bangor where I was taught to milk and look after the dairy. On the first day I was taken into the cowshed and shown how to milk by hand. I only got half a pint out and when they let the cow out she walked with a limp. I thought I had hurt her – I hadn't though, she always walked like that! Next morning I had to go to the doctor's as I couldn't move my fingers and arms; the doctor informed me I was using muscles I had not used before. I couldn't hold a cup or knife and fork for a week and my mother had to feed me.

I had to wash the milk bottles and milking machine twice every day and put them in the sterilizer and steam them for 15 minutes. We milked three times a day which meant getting up at 5.30am in order to start milking at 6.00, we then milked again at 12.00 noon and 6.00pm. The milk was TT.

I did two years at Lonisaf then my mother had a breakdown and had to go into hospital while we were on leave in London. I had to leave the Land Army to look after my sister in Whipps Cross Home. The bombing got so bad we were evacuated to Tempsford. It was not long before I was asked to help on Lambscourt Farm so I rejoined the Land Army. I milked and helped in the fields; the milk was taken to Tempsford Aerodrome every day by horse and cart then the waste from the cookhouse was brought back and cooked every day for the pigs. The geese would wait until I had got both hands full and then come up behind and peck me.

We worked in the fields by Tempsford aerodrome, not

knowing what was going on there. We learnt after the war people were being taken over to France to work with the Resistance.

In August 1945 I married one of my boss's sons, Mont, and went to live in the farm cottage called Pleasant Cottage.'

'Whilst serving in the Land Army, I was working on a rather remote farm with no mains facilities. The cooking was done on a large old fashioned range, which intrigued the three young evacuees who were living on the farm. They were always impressing on us "We have got gas". The farmer's wife had allocated them all little chores.

The eldest boy, Harry, was to always make sure the wood box was kept full, as she explained to them if the fire went out there would be no hot meals. One day she had killed a hen. After plucking and drawing it, she was singeing the down feathers with a candle. The younger boy came in and looked at her open mouthed. Then he glanced at the wood box which happened to be empty.

He turned on his heel and rushed out of the kitchen shouting "Harry, Harry, you forgot to fill the wood box, missus is cooking the chicken with a candle."'

'During the Second World War I left my home in London to join the Women's Land Army. Our job was to replace the male farmworkers who had been called up by the army, navy or the airforce. What a different sort of life this was for me! There I was in the south east of London working in a biscuit factory packing iron rations for the troops one minute and the next miles out in the country, hoeing, pulling sugar beet and all sorts of outdoor jobs I had never experienced before. I travelled from Kings Cross to Kettering and from there was picked up in a van by the forewoman to a big country house which had been turned into a hostel for the girls; we were looked after by a female warden. After a night's sleep we were taken to our farm and left there to work for the day until the lorry picked us up at the end of the day. There we were as green as grass trying to get used to hoes, pitchforks and the blisters! We were to find muscles we never knew we had and we were glad when we saw the lorry each evening.

One day the farmer gave me the job of feeding his pig. I went to the house to collect a bucket of pigswill from the farmer's wife, a handful of meal was stirred in with a big stick and all was poured into the trough. I felt very important being chosen to do this until the next morning when we arrived for work. There was the farmer hopping mad accusing me of killing his pig. I explained that I had carried out his instructions to the letter. Fortunately a post mortem revealed that there had been a pot scourer in the swill!

As life went on I learnt many jobs on the farm and began to enjoy living in the country and in 1949 married, and helped my husband to run a smallholding. I often think about my time in the Land Army and the friendships made and the fun we had together and despite all the hardships suffered I would not change that time for anything.'

'Whilst working in the Women's Land Army during the war, us hitherto helpless females were sent with the young farmhands to drive the horse-drawn harvest carts.

On my first day the horse I was leading stopped several times in the length of one field.

"Sid", I asked the horse-keeper's son, "Why does he keep stopping?"

Sid shouted back that he wanted to water. Thinking he meant the horse was thirsty I innocently inquired where I should take him. This met with gales of laughter.'

'When I first came to Tempsford in 1944 as a Land Army girl, I thought what a nice village it was, a lot of thatched cottages and houses, a proper little village. I remember when I reached the farm where I was to work, the yard was full of children and I thought to myself "It's true what they say about farmers having lots of children" but I was to learn later that they were the children from the village. The farmer did however have four children of his own, as did his younger brother who was a partner in the farm.

Before I came to Tempsford, I did my training at a hostel in Toddington. We had fun there but the work was very hard as well. The first day I was to milk a cow (of which I knew nothing at all), the supervisor in charge said to the other girls, with a grin, "I think Dorothy can milk the heifer". I soon found out what the grin was for; having managed to get over half a bucket of milk, she gave such a kick I lost all the milk that I had worked so hard for, down the gully. The reason being she was a first time calver and very nervous, but I got on OK after that. The first time I had to lead a horse and cart through a gate, it ended up with one wheel on one side of the gate-post and the cart on the other. Being frightened of horses I had been too busy watching his "feet". We had to take the horse out of the cart to free it, you can guess I wasn't very popular. Another thing we had to do was to lead the bull in from the gate by his halter, which I refused to do, I was only a raw recruit at the time, but for all of that I was passed a fully fledged "Land Girl" at the end of my training.

Back to Tempsford. The farm that I went to had a village girl working there as well and we got on well together. My job apart from milking and keeping the cow-shed and dairy very clean, and mixing their feed, was to do the milk-round. No I couldn't drive, it was done on a bicycle, with a churn on each handlebar. Two measures, one for a pint and another for half a pint. Sometimes I would be told that I had given short measure, which I am sure that I hadn't but I topped the jug up to save any trouble. I only had one mishap with the churns and that was trying to get the bicycle through the small gate at the level-crossing, without taking them off the handlebars first, and I lost one by it falling off. I just stood there and watched the milk flowing down the road. I had to finish the round with the afternoon milking, I can't remember if I told the "Boss". There was one lady who always had a cup of hot cocoa for me when I delivered her milk. We also had to drive the cows and the bull along the road to their field in the morning and bring them back in the afternoon. So long as the bull had his "lady" friends with him he was alright, but I still kept my eye on him!

As well as looking after the cows, I also did field work,

211

which included hoeing and stacking corn sheaves. At one time I did it with barley; I didn't think about the new cardigan I had on at the time, until I was finished. The only way to get rid of the barley ears from the wool was to unpick it, needless to say it was never reknitted. Corn was put through a threshing machine and I always got the job of bagging the chaff up, which is the husks off the corn, a very dusty job. Harvest is much easier today. Haymaking, which was very different in those days, was cut and stacked loose, unlike today when it is baled up and much easier to handle.

The air force was in Tempsford during the war years and it made the village a lively place, always a sing-song in the pubs and dances held in the Stuart Memorial Hall were a regular thing. Those were the days.

I later married one of the farmer's sons and came out of the Land Army in 1947, but my work on the land was by no means over . . .'

MAKING DO

Whether it was stretching the rations out to last the week, or going back to pony and trap to get into town, local people used their ingenuity to get through the long war years. And at last it was time to celebrate the Peace, and though the story of the weekend to remember comes

212

from a lady who was then living in Lancashire, it stands for all those youngsters who finally found the future worth contemplating.

STRETCHING THE RATIONS

'Quite a few American servicemen came over to Stevington from Alconbury to attend chapel on a Sunday evening. Families in the village would entertain them to tea before chapel. The minister had a contact with the chaplain at Alconbury through being a chaplain himself during the First World War. Evacuees also came, from London first of all, and then other parts of the country. There were also land girls on two of the farms and Italian prisoners also came to work on the farms in Stevington.

We were able to eke out our rationing by keeping pigs in the back gardens along with chickens and were able to get a bit of home-made butter from the farm. Pigs were killed every Friday morning on the premises which is now the post office. Red Cross classes were held every week in the chapel. Each week different work was carried out according to the war requirements. Making bandages, pyjamas for injured service men, snow suits for service personnel going to Norway, rush jobs for shrouds following heavy bombing raids, were some of the jobs accomplished on these evenings. Our mothers also spent hours knitting socks, gloves, scarves, balaclavas, etc for the "Comforts for the Forces" effort. We also had ARP classes – lectures and practises in the club room and school and then someone from "Shire Hall" came and tested us and issued us with certificates.'

'During the war most families in Little Staughton had evacuees and rations were such that we had to have bread and Oxo every night for our supper. Shopping was not easy; very few families had a car and anyway petrol was scarce. There was a local bus to go to Bedford market on Wednesday or to St Neots market on Thursday, or you used a bicycle. We used to collect our daily milk in cans from a local farm. Our village school was a good one, but more often than not the children wore hand-me-downs. In the winter we often had to do running on the spot just to keep warm.'

'When David married Daisy in February 1942 there was thick snow in Bletsoe and the bride, who worked at the rectory, found it difficult to walk to the church. The wedding cake was a sponge, with a carefully made white cardboard cover to make it look like a proper wedding cake.'

'I was born in Norfolk, where one of the hundreds of traditions was the "Shortcake" – a confection of very short pastry, covered in currants and sugar, folded together, rolled out again, cut into oblongs and baked on a tray.

Of course, during the war when currants disappeared from the market place, this was a "disaster" along with all the air raids. I think it was 1941 when the military appeared and told my mother that they proposed to dig out our front garden hedge and install three gun positions as our house was situated very strategically at the junction of five main roads, also we had a barrage balloon in our back garden. We were not sure whether we felt protected or targeted.

I digress! To camouflage the gun emplacements, the army covered them with elderberry bushes, laden with berries. For tea that very evening appeared a cake-plate laden with "Shortcake". It was not until they all were eaten that anyone began to query where they came from – was the war over? had rationing finished? had Mother done something awful with the coupons? Nothing so exciting – the elderberries had been collected from the bushes, dried in the oven and replaced the currants in the confection – delicious!'

'During the war there were about six evacuees sent to Tingrith and Land Army girls to work on the farms. After I married and moved to the farm we had prisoners from Germany to help us. They were brought and collected each day.

Of course food was rationed during the war and you were allowed 2oz corned beef with the meat ration. I very often made a dumpling with potato and onion. If we didn't have any suet for the crust we would make it with mashed potato, margarine and flour but at least it was a nice hot meal. During this time villagers were better off than people in the town as everybody helped each other with fresh eggs and bacon.

The village pub was a meeting place for men, as before the war it was unheard of for a woman to enter. After the war men and women went every Saturday night and had a good sing song.'

LOSING OUR HOME

'My husband Stan and I went to live at Little Staughton in 1933. We bought a house at Top End next to a pub called The Shoulder of Mutton, which was opposite Mr Ruff's garage and several houses. There were also houses near us and further down the road another pub called The Bushell and Strike.

We had oil lamps and had to fetch water from a pump at the end of Wickey Lane. We also had a wireless set which ran on a battery which had to be charged every week. Later on water came to the village and we had a standpipe opposite our house.

My husband tried his hand at selling drapery, because there was a slump at the time. His new venture prospered and he travelled all around the local villages and soon became well known. He had an old van, nothing posh then. The older women were so pleased to be able to buy their fleecy-lined underwear, jumpers, cardigans, sheets and pillowcases and numerous other things. He was almost chased after when "nylons" came on the scene. The men, mostly farm workers, bought their shirts, corduroy trousers, wellington boots, long pants and vests from him.

His business expanded so he bought a new van and went further out to Woburn, Lidlington, and other places. Then came the war and everything had to be sold on coupons, but we managed to buy stock from our London wholesalers by taking them some lovely new laid eggs.

Unfortunately, in about 1942 a bulldozer came and knocked down our house and all the others, about 20. Over the back, in our field, with masses of concrete, runways and buildings, we watched the start of an aerodrome.'

A CHILD'S VIEW

'I don't remember a lot about the war but what I do remember is a large map on the wall of Grandfather's

216

house (where we lived whilst father was away at the war) with a lot of pink on it and all sitting round in silence listening to the radio, where nobody dared utter or make the minutest noise; the flags that were systematically moved as a result of the broadcast and a stern looking Grandfather with a beard. And there was the lorry passing us outside the police station and the American soldiers throwing oranges at us for us to scramble about picking them up – such excitement! And hiding in my aunt's cupboard under the stairs in Rushden when the air raid sirens went off. And taking gas masks to school and practising getting them on – I could do it today – chin thrust forward and in and then pull on! And my Dad coming home – a lovely man with a laugh and a pipe!'

GETTING ABOUT

'Living in the country during and for quite a time after the Second World War was not too easy, especially shopping etc. The nearest shop to where I lived was three miles away. Petrol was severely rationed, so it was either Shanks's pony or on a bicycle for me. I used to cycle to the town at least twice a week as I was catering for seven people, two of whom were evacuees, and you really cannot carry very much on a bicycle. It was lovely going, as it was downhill most of the way but the return journey was not so pleasant cycling uphill with all the shopping! I used to cycle to the WI at night and in the winter going past the dense woods was very scary especially as the owls hooted, I was always glad to get home.

When our children had to start school in 1942 we

decided to buy a pony and buggy, which compared to the bicycle was a very comfortable commodity. The buggy was a very light vehicle for one or two persons, but ours often carried four children and myself, packed in too tight to fall out. George the pony was a strong little animal and did his job willingly. When I went shopping with him I would sit outside and wait until the shopkeeper came out for my order, as there were no lamp posts to tie the pony up to. George had one fault which was very embarrassing, he would always wait until we got on the narrow St Neots bridge to stop and relieve himself, holding up all the traffic; he just would not move until he was finished! I was involved with WVS work helping at a canteen on the market square for the American servicemen. I used to drive George to the Cross Keys pub in St Neots and for sixpence the pony would be taken out of the buggy, put in a stall and whatever time I wanted him he was always ready, harnessed up again by a dear old man who had once been an ostler and it seemed to delight him to do this job. We eventually purchased a second hand Austin Seven for under £40 which used very little petrol – I often wish I had it now!'

CELEBRATING PEACE

'I was a teenager in 1945 when we were all celebrating the outbreak of peace. There were parties and hopes-for-the-future. The weekend after the big Services Victory parade in Hyde Park, it was the turn of the Rangers, Sea, Land and Air. From all over Britain we converged on London for the weekend of our lives.

A select few from my Sea Ranger Company in Lancashire

were chosen to attend. For weeks we were drilled by a Sergeant – ex-army – who despaired of us ever learning how to Right Turn and Form Fours. Then there was much washing and ironing of uniforms, polishing of shoes and badges and gathering of food to last us on our six hour train journey to London.

I don't remember anything about the journey, but we finally arrived at Clapham South tube station where hundreds of three-tiered bunks had been placed in the underground passages. They had been used during the war to accommodate the homeless. We were allocated our berths, fed on rather dry bread sandwiches and told to retire. This was great fun – three-tiered bunks make super gymnastic apparatus. We eventually went to sleep to be awakened by the strident tones of a male voice telling South West Yorkshire to "Please get up and perform your ablutions, girls" and would the rest of us *stay put* until we were called.

After a breakfast of boiled eggs – an unexpected treat, because eggs were severely rationed – we were taken to our various mustering points. Ours was Wellington Barracks. The soldiers had been confined to barracks, and spent the next few hours calling out of the windows in high falsetto voices such witticisms as "Form Fours!" and "Quick March, girls". Of course, we ignored them!

We were inspected by some Guiders and then marched to Hyde Park. Naturally, the Sea Rangers looked the best in their navy skirts, white cotton "rowing vests", black ties (these were triangular and worn with the point at the back of the neck) and our special Sea Ranger hats. We carried navy raincoats over our arms. However, as we waited at the entrance to Hyde Park, down came the rain: gallons and gallons of it. The order came, "Put on raincoats". Still it rained. Then, just as we were about to march off, the sun came out. "Take off raincoats." Oh dear! In those days, dyes weren't as "fixed" as they are today and our lovely white shirts were all stained blue across the shoulders.

Nevertheless, steaming gently in the sunshine, we marched bravely on, 10,000 Rangers striding out. "Eyes right!" There they were – Princesses Elizabeth and Margaret Rose taking the salute, in their Sea Ranger uniforms (of course, they belonged to the Senior Service, like us). Hadn't Elizabeth got a lot of lipstick on! Perhaps it was for the cameras.

In the evening we met up again in the Royal Albert Hall. One of our Crew had been chosen to carry the Flag for Lancashire. We basked in reflected glory. Princess Margaret was the guest of honour and we were rather disappointed because she looked just like one of us in her uniform. What had we expected? A tiara?

I think we all slept on the journey home, to emerge bleary eyed next day at our home station.

But what a weekend to remember.'

HIGHDAYS & HOLIDAYS

MAKING OUR OWN ENTERTAINMENT

In the days before television, and even radio, people made their own entertainment in school rooms and village halls across the county. They got together to put on plays and concerts, to play whist and dance the night away, to sing and to play musical instruments. The amount of talent to be found in even small villages was astounding. If sport was your fancy, you could indulge that too, with tennis, cricket, swimming and skating. People may not have had as much leisure time in the past, but they certainly made the most of what they had.

CONCERTS, PLAYS AND FILM SHOWS

'The entertainment we enjoyed at Houghton Conquest was mostly brought to us, and was held in what was called the Old School Church Rooms, situated in the middle of the village above the almshouses.

One concert party was called "The Jabberwoks" with Tom Swann comedian, Lily Lee, Dainty Lichfield soprano and the Martin Bros. They sang songs such as "Dancing with my shadow", "Dear little jammy face" and "My little grey home in the west". Tom Swann the comedian would tell really corny jokes, and his face was like rubber, he could pull it in all shapes, but he made us laugh.

Mr Edward Pearce was the magician and always got the most applause, he happened to be our church organist, and was exceptionally good at making things disappear and reappear; he went on to become a member of the Inner Magic Circle in London.

Once a year the Co-op held a social evening. This was free to all, and we really enjoyed the games and the food that was provided for us. We won prizes, these were of course small samples of Co-op products, but we were delighted if we won something.

Also once a year the Caravan Mission Society would put up a tent in a field in Rectory Lane. Here we were taught choruses, and we sang the "Books of the Bible" to the tune of "Sun of my soul", I can still remember them by heart, once taught never forgotten.

Of course we did have local talent and these concerts were impromptu, if you could entertain in any way you did it. Bill Smart and Tom Smart had fine singing voices as did Mrs Freda Gilbert. These were good times, and I can look back and say, they were "The Good Old Days".'

'Between the wars, people living in the country had to more or less make their own entertainment. At Salford we had great fun at social evenings in the school room. These were attended by practically everyone, adults and children, and took the form of singing, recitation, small sketches, the odd dance and maybe a rendering on a musical instrument. Sometimes a travelling player would come and hire the school room for a magic lantern show, taking us into the world of make believe. Towards the end of the 1930s a cinema was built at Cranfield, the next village, and people began to cycle the three miles to go to the pictures. Before that the nearest cinema was at Bletchley or Newport Pagnell, a distance of six or seven miles. Once a week young men met in the village hall to play billiards or table tennis, but there were no such delights for the young women.'

'There was always a procession of people walking over Dunstable Downs every Sunday afternoon – there was much more walking then than there is now. Other entertainments in Dunstable included dancing, Saturday morning cinema, roller skating at the Half Moon rink and swimming at the California pool.'

'My mother joined Wootton WI in the early 1920s and it was very popular with many women in the village. The president at that time was Mrs Squire, who was the vicar's wife. She was a small lady, rather plump, with white hair. But more especially, she was an accomplished pianist and organist, also a very good conductor.

Apart from monthly meetings, Friday night was folk night, when we gathered in the church room for folk songs and country dancing. We had a very good choir, and always competed at the Bedford Eisteddfod where we won many prizes. People loved to watch Mrs Squire when she was conducting us, and would crowd into the hall to see the little woman perform.

Wootton WI also had a drama group, who would put on a performance each year. My mother had a very good soprano voice, and would sing a solo, as well as perform in the current play. Rehearsals were often performed at our house, and my brother and I were allowed to sit up late to watch.

There was a lady called Miss Glennie, who lived in London but came to the vicarage for a holiday for a few weeks at a time. She would write an old-time musical play for the WI to perform. This play would be performed in the summertime, on one of the big lawns at the vicarage. I was in one of the very first ones she wrote, and I played the part of the squire's little boy, kidnapped by a roving pedlar. The best part was that at each performance, he gave me a lollipop from his tray of wares!

The garden at the vicarage was almost like a stage, as the big french windows of the drawing room, when opened, gave entrance to a long sloping lawn. Also there was a long trellised walk on the right-hand side, covered in rambling roses, which gave another entrance to the lawn – or stage as it was. On the left-hand side, under a huge chestnut tree, sat our audience.

Our author always had a good plot for us to act, and brought in lots of songs and country dancing.'

'When the magic lantern came to the church room in Stevington the entry fee was a halfpenny – it didn't come very often, families with several children found it too expensive, but we always went.'

'We used to arrange little concerts in our garden at Bromham before the war. I had to sing and dance with my friend Vera and I enjoyed the chance to show off. Film shows in the garage of Mr Walker's shop were a great event and were packed with us children.'

'There were three cinemas in Leighton Buzzard at one

time – the Grand which is now a car salesroom, the Oriel which is now a supermarket, and the Old Vic which was later used for concert parties and dances but has now given way to the ring road.'

'A dancing class known as the "Six penny hop" was held in the Assembly Rooms at Potton behind the Rose and Crown. It was organised by Madge Hibbs and Doris Campling. Jimmy Yorke from Sandy played the piano. The last dance was always the Lancers and the boys were told not to lift the girls off their feet, but they didn't listen! People came from nearby villages. We all knew each other and it was good natured fun.'

'In my younger days we used to make our own entertainment. When I was 15 together with others, a band was formed called "The Colmworth Review Band". Five of us played in the band which consisted of piano, drums, first and second fiddle and I played the banjo. We practised in the evenings after working all day, concentrating mainly on all the popular dance tunes of the 1920s and 1930s. Most Friday and Saturday nights we would play for local dances.

We were very much in demand and would often travel anything from five to 15 miles to perform in neighbouring villages. We used a motor bike to get around until we could afford a car, our first car being a two seater tourer, very cramped for four people! Some of the social evenings started with a whist drive followed by dancing for which we would play, on these occasions our pay was £1. For a whole evening of dancing we received 25 shillings and this fee was to be shared between the five of us of course. On summer afternoons we would often be invited to play at village fetes, when the event would finish up with a dance in the evening, for which we were paid £2.

All this was before the Second World War and I gave up playing when my daughter was born in 1938.'

'Sometimes on a Saturday between the wars we would ride our bikes to Bedford to play cricket, then we would go to the pictures or the theatre in the evening. One Saturday we had been playing there and we had a bit of tea in the Silver Grill which used to be in Bedford High Street. You could get a plate of ham for just over a shilling. Another time we went to the second house theatre. It must have been about half past ten when we came out and we had to walk about a mile to where we left our bikes at a pub yard called the Blacksmith's Arms. There used to be hundreds of people put their bikes up there, now there's none at all. After we got our bikes I had got six miles to bike home to Cople and another two miles on from the village to our farm.

There is a big hill before you get to our farm gate and I remember pedalling along up the hill very tired. We had only got oil lamps on our bikes then and both of them had run out of oil. It was pitch dark, and suddenly a bright light shone in my face and with that light there was the village policeman. He had been to meet the other constable from Northill and was on his way back to Cople. Well, I should think he stood there talking to me for about an hour and a half and I wanted to get home to bed but never once did he say anything about my lights. Then when he was starting off, he turned to me and said "You know, Arch, a couple of nice rabbits would be very nice", so I had to get them as soon as I could.

227

He used to have a little brown dog when he was on his beat and it would be about 40 or 50 yards in front of him, so if you hadn't got a light you could either get off and walk or turn back. I can't ever remember him summonsing anyone – he used to make things right with a few pints of beer.

When we got home on Saturday nights we used to have fresh herrings or sausages for supper. They were kept warm in the oven and if you were home first you had the largest lot. Then we put on the headphones and listened to the dance music on the wireless; that's when they first came out and they were called a cat's whisker.'

LEIGHTON BUZZARD EISTEDDFOD

'One of the best memories of my younger years happened during the 1930s. Each springtime an Eisteddfod was held in the Corn Exchange at Leighton Buzzard, which was arranged by the Methodist church and took place over two weeks. There were classes for anyone who had any talent, whether it be cooking or art or singing and the playing of musical instruments. Separate evenings were held for each group of instruments, wind, string, and pianoforte, also male voices and female voices and choirs. Elocution was very popular too.

Well known adjudicators were there to judge each class and much interest was shown by the members of the audiences, choosing which entry *they* thought should be placed first, which needless to say, did not always agree with the adjudicator. People of all ages from the very young to the more mature would take part in their appropriate section, which made good training for children later in their lives to perform in public. The last two nights of the Eisteddfod were devoted to performances by all the first prize winners.

Around May time most of the local chapels would hold their Sunday school Anniversaries. All the girls would wear their best dresses and pretty hats and the boys were in their suits. The scent of lilies of the valley brings back happy memories of those days. Many members of the congregation would wear sprays of these flowers in their buttonholes. The services those days were arranged by the Sunday school and members were chosen to be soloists. The old Wesleyan Methodist church in Hockliffe Street would hold around 1,500 people with more extra seating having to be brought in. It was a nerve racking time when one had to stand up and sing.'

PRE-WAR PARTIES

'I was born two months after the armistice that ended the First World War. In some ways our lives linked with the pre-war days. I remember particularly the dance Roger de Coverley that always ended our parties. The preparation for our parties, which celebrated Christmas, New Year and Birthday rolled into one, was considerable. A date was fixed, guests listed, invitations carefully penned in best handwriting and in formal style "E and B request the pleasure of the company of . . . etc." Although we were very young, all the proprieties were observed and we learned early the French for RSVP. These were hand delivered as most friends lived nearby, and anyway, post at a penny ha' penny was an unnecessary expense!

Mother had a busy time in the kitchen, preparing cakes –

coconut pyramids, and iced sponges cut into squares, pink icing with half a glace cherry and chocolate icing with half a blanched almond. Jellies were made and blancmanges. I remember one particular delight; half orange skins were saved, filled with orange jelly and then cut in half. They were eaten like a quartered orange, and many a sticky face resulted. There were sandwiches too, and scones.

My sister and I made a list of games and prepared competitions well in advance. There would be a wall competition to fill the times of arrivals, a "musical" parcel, papers cut and pencils sharpened for paper games like the hilarious Consequences and the more difficult alphabetical Bird, Beast and Fish. Prizes and any other items needed were prepared and placed on the top of the piano out of harm's way.

Finally the day arrived. A large oak log fire was lit to warm the cold north-facing front room. We waited in our party dresses, our eyes sparkling with excitement, for the guests to arrive. Most walked and were brought by a parent. Mufflers and boots were taken off and pretty slippers and light shoes put on. There was a lot of laughter and chatter as the programme got under way. Every moment was filled with activity.

As I reach into my memories for the games I am amazed at the variety we played over the years. My Friend's Chair, Postman's Knock, Poor Puss (trying not to laugh), Hunt the Thimble, Musical Bumps, Blind Man's Buff, General Post, Forfeits, Consequences, Pinning a Tail on the Donkey, Oranges and Lemons, Bob Apple (in the bathroom) or Apple on a String.

As we grew older, more sophisticated games were chosen; Sardines and Murder when the whole house was used; Winking – a delightful excuse for those first early "primrose" kisses; Musical Laps in place of the infantile Bumps, and Charades. Another rumbustious activity was Cockfighting. The contestants sat on the floor opposite each other, trussed up with wrists and ankles tied and a walking stick pushed through elbows and under the knees, and with toes just touching. The object was to push your opponent off balance, where he or she remained until righted by the onlookers.

When tea was served, it was orderly and sedate. The table was attractively laid out and if extra seating was needed Father made a form with a plank of wood between two chairs. Cushions were placed to protect little bare legs from the rough wood. Grace was said and then everyone's needs were attended to; the shy ones encouraged to tuck in and a gentle restraint to any who might eat too much. There were crackers or snowballs with little gifts.

Near the end of the earlier parties my father did his "act". He dressed up as a rotund taxi driver, wearing his old RNAS peaked cap and a well padded tummy. He said he'd come to take so-and-so home. At first there was slight consternation, and then, as the trick was realised, there was a great pummelling of the padded "tum" and much laughter and relief all round. The party was not quite over! The end always followed the same formula. Roger de Coverley, Mother at the piano, and then Auld Lang Syne. In 1940 I celebrated my 21st and it was the end of party time. Already the boys had been posted round the world in Army, Navy and RAF. But we all had the memories of those wonderful friendly times to sustain us during the long years of wartime separation.'

AUTOGRAPH HUNTING

'A popular custom in the 1920s was collecting autographs. Most people had these little albums given to them into which friends and relations wrote verses or did drawings. These are two such verses found in an old album which are typical of the time.

"Look not for the faults as you go through life,
And even when you find them,
Tis wise and kind to be somewhat blind,
And look for the virtues behind them."

And the following by Charles Kingsley.

"Be good sweet maid – and let who will be clever;
Do lovely things, not dream them all day long;
And so make Life, and Death, and that For Ever
One grand sweet song."

SPORTS FOR ALL

'During very cold weather a field on the outskirts of Leighton Buzzard, known as Bate's Mill, was flooded and many of the young people would go skating there. A flooded pit known as The Spinney Pool was the only public swimming pool we had and many people used it. A new pool was built in the 1930s at the Cedars Grammar School for the use of the pupils.'

'In the winter at Sharnbrook the fields by the river were flooded between Felmersham and Ouse Manor and skating took place in Big Meadow. Mother and most of the other youngsters had skates.'

'In such a small town as Luton in the 1910s everyone knew each other. Walking and picnicking in the country, taking cricket stumps and balls etc was all the rage. Doris tells an interesting story regarding the swimming pool then situated in Waller Street, Luton. When the swimming pool was first opened around 1916 (slipper baths and separate pools opened in 1872) the sexes were segregated – special hours for women and men, and when finally mixed bathing was allowed, this was done under strict supervision as to behaviour. To the extent that the local Councillors used to inspect the pool to make certain that swimmers behaved themselves! Anyone standing on the side of the pool was told to get into the pool, and swimming costumes with sleeves had to be worn for decency!

Entertainment at home consisted of card games of every kind and dominoes, and Doris can remember her parents organising whist drives with prizes in their home.

Doris's family always had a yearly outing on the train to a pantomime at Drury Lane in February. Wind up gramophones were coming in and silent cinema was also on the horizon (the Anglo-American Electric Theatre opened in Gordon Street in 1909, followed by the Picturedrome in Park Street in 1911 and Plaza and Wellington both in 1912).'

'Before the war there was a tennis club in Stevington village, started by the student pastor at the chapel, Stanley Reed. Matches were played against teams from Bedford Adults School, Clapham, Kempston East Methodist Chapel, St Mary's Wesleyan, Southend Methodist (in Bedford), Bedford Co-op, Cryselco, Houghton Conquest and Lynton

Works. Once the war came the three grass courts had to be ploughed up for agricultural use.'

'One of the main sports for men at Dean was cricket, and they had a formidable team between the wars. There was also a good football team very well supported. Several of the larger houses had tennis courts which they opened to the village once a week. Many tournaments were played against nearby villages. A hockey team for girls took them to Kimbolton, Huntingdon, Bedford and local villages.'

'At our cricket pitch in Roxton Park in the 1940s only the table was fenced in to keep off the sheep and cattle. It was not unusual for the ball to splosh in a cow pat, much to the delight of the rest of the team. "Come on," was their cry, "pick the ball up and get it back to the keeper", as one gingerly wiped the cow-muck off. Often a field was left for hay. I recall in about 1955 going to Cople to play on their former pitch, where one entered the field, climbed over a stile, and it was just like looking down into a swimming pool, with tall grass surrounding the cricket table. One of our batsmen ran five runs until "lost ball" was called, with the ball barely hit off the table.'

MEMORABLE OCCASIONS

Certain events and celebrations stick in the memory, such as Royal jubilees and coronations, or seeing the

first aeroplanes or the great R101 airship, or going to Wembley to watch a rodeo or the Cup Final. Lloyd George even made one election memorable!

AEROPLANES AND AIRSHIPS

'In about 1911 or 1912 we were taken to the Race Meadow on the Ampthill Road to see two aeroplanes which were racing from near London to the Midlands and back. They had to come down to refuel. I think all of Bedford and Kempston were there as we had never seen an aeroplane before. Graham White flew an aeroplane which looked like a sort of bamboo cage with his legs dangling below. My father was very scornful but it didn't stop him going to see it.'

'One of my earliest memories dates back to 1911, on the day that Graham White, one of the first "Flying Men", landed his aeroplane in a cornfield by Biddenham church. I was only three years old at the time, and it was a very long walk from Beverley Crescent, Bedford. Thousands of people came from miles around to see the first aeroplane, and the picture of it will remain in my mind for ever.'

'Before Mr Shuttleworth had the aerodrome made at Old Warden he used to keep two planes in one of the fields at Moxhill Farm, where there was plenty of space and no trees in the way. He used to come across the fields on an old motor bike when he wanted to go for a trip, all through his own estate. When he had gone up in one of his aeroplanes I used to get on his motor bike and have a good old spin round the meadows; whether he saw me I don't know but he never said anything about it.

I was down in the field one Sunday morning when Mr Shuttleworth came for a flight and he asked me if I would like to go up for a ride. I said yes, I would, and I got in. It was a two seater and I remember him strapping me in and he said "I don't want you to fall out as it would be a horrible mess to clear up on a Sunday!" It was my first trip in a plane and we were up for about 20 minutes. Things looked very different from above and the houses looked so small. I liked it all right when we were going up, but when he did a few tricks I didn't think much to it, it made me feel very sick. When we landed there were several boys there from the farm cottages and he took them all up one at a time; he was a very nice man. On another occasion when my father was down the field he took him up for a trip too. It was the only time my father went up for he was getting on a bit in years, but he said he enjoyed it.

Then Mr Shuttleworth joined the Royal Air Force and unfortunately he was killed when the bomber he was in crashed into a mountain. It was a very sad day for the whole estate.

Before we were married my wife worked in the canteen up Cardington camp when they were building the R101 airship, so she knew all the crew as they used to come in for meals. I remember her telling me that one of them always came in for a bacon sandwich and the morning before they took off on their last flight he said to my wife, "I'll have a bacon sandwich – it will be the last one I shall have" and he was right. I went to meet her from work that evening and I was in the camp when the airship took off. It didn't seem to me as if it was

236

going very well. Then we went off towards Bedford on the old motor bike and as we went along the airship passed overhead.

As we all know, it crashed in flames in France, killing nearly all the crew, two of them from the village of Cardington. I knew them very well as I used to play football with them in the village team, but they didn't come back and it was a very sad day for everyone. I went to see them buried in one big grave at Cardington cemetery. There were thousands of people there from all over the country and some from abroad. The Royal Air Force bands were there and the trumpeters played the Last Post. And that was the end of airships of any size at Cardington, although they have made several small ones.'

LLOYD GEORGE

'One of my earliest and most vivid childhood recollections is, when I was seven, being taken by my grandfather to see Lloyd George. He was on a whistle-stop tour, prior to a general election. His car stopped in the village square and I can see him as if it were yesterday, with his long white hair and Welsh tweed cape. I remember standing mesmerised as he addressed the crowd.

The election day was a holiday for the school children. There was great excitement the afternoon before when a huge traction engine arrived outside the school, towing a shepherd's lambing hut. It was to be the local committee room and getting it into position was a major operation. Next morning was bitterly cold so the stove was lit but a gale blew up and, to this day, I can see the smoke billowing out of the open door as well as from the chimney, with the poor tellers standing outside, shivering in the cold.'

OFF TO WEMBLEY

'I went to Wembley when the rodeo was on and enjoyed it very much, seeing the cowboys trick riding and roping and throwing the steers. They used to chase the steers up the arena on horseback and then dive off the horses onto the steer's horns and twist their necks round till they pulled them to the ground. Then they would tie them up so they couldn't get up and the one who did it the quickest was the winner. Then they had broncho busting. They made the horses buck by tying a cord right round their flanks and when a cowboy had ridden his time another would ride up and undo the cord at the top of the horse's flanks and he would stop bucking at once. I thought that was a bit cruel. I remember some of the cowboys' names, such as Frank McCorral and Powder River Thompson, but not all of them.

On the next Monday morning I went with one of our chaps to fetch a pony which had been for a rest on another farm after a week on the milk float. I thought I would be a bit clever and I said to my mate "I didn't go to Wembley for nothing, I'll show you how the cowboys ride." I had only got a hemp halter on the horse and just one rein so I jumped on its back, gave it a touch with the rein and away it went, and the next thing I knew I was sailing through the air. I don't think I would have made a very good cowboy, but when you are young you like to try anything for a bit of fun. By the way, the pony was home long before us.

I also went to Wembley when the circus was on. There were three rings going all at once. But what I liked best was when I had the good fortune to get a ticket for the Cup Final at Wembley between Preston Northend and Sunderland. It was a wonderful sight with the bands playing and all the singing before the start, especially when the band played Abide With Me. It was a very touching scene when everybody stood up and took their hats off.'

ROYAL CELEBRATIONS

'Coronations and Queen Victoria's Jubilee were all celebrated at Roxton with teas for the children and meat teas for the adults, followed by sports. A greasy pig was grappled for at the Jubilee and one lady lost her wedding ring in a futile attempt to catch it.'

'Two events stick out in my mind, George V's Silver Jubilee on 6th May 1935 and George VI's Coronation celebrated on 12th May 1937.

These were entirely village affairs taking up the whole day, starting with a service in Salford church in the morning then home for dinner (lunch was for the rich). In the afternoon we all assembled in the Manor Field for the Fancy Dress Parade. Adults as well as children dressed up and prizes were given for the best costumes. After this the races got under way – running, sack, egg and spoon, slow bicycle race and a run round the village.

At four o'clock we all repaired to the school room for a sit down tea. The King's health was drunk in tea or home-made lemonade.

Then it was back to the field for more races and a cricket match between men and women. Invariably the men won but they had to bat left handed.

The climax came about eight o'clock when the prizes were presented and each child received a souvenir. For the Silver Jubilee we had a cup and saucer with the King and Queen painted on the cup and for the Coronation a mug with the head of George VI on.

The money for these jollifications had been collected weekly from each family, the amount according to the ability to pay.

We were given a day off school when the dukes of Kent and Gloucester were married but as these events took place in November no special celebration was arranged.'

'We had a television set especially for the Coronation of Elizabeth II in 1953. My aunt and uncle came to see it with us and I had a tin of toffees with the Queen on the lid. In the afternoon there was a fancy dress competition for the children of Sharnbrook village. I went as a hula hula girl with brown stage make up on and a grass skirt. Nigel Blood won, dressed as a Guardsman with a lovely busby his mother had made.'

THROUGH THE YEAR

From Plough Monday through the year round to Christmas again, every village and town in Bedfordshire

celebrated the annual holidays and occasions. Many are still celebrated today, though Empire Day on 24th May, once a highlight of the year for schoolchildren throughout the country, has gone the way of the British Empire it celebrated, and Boat Race Day no longer commands the intense interest it once produced.

PLOUGH MONDAY

'At Stevington the first Monday in January, Plough Monday, was always celebrated. After finishing the winter ploughing the boys would black their faces and go round the village rattling a tin and singing – money for their beer. We children joined in, dressing in rags and blacking our faces, and we knocked on doors asking "Tink boy, plough boy, gi's penny ha'penny" (or in other words, "Think of the poor plough boy, give us a penny ha'penny").'

BOAT RACE DAY

'Whether it was because Bedford was a rowing town, or perhaps it was the same everywhere, but you just had to support either Oxford or Cambridge in the Boat Race. Traders would be on the market selling favours in either light or dark blue. The outcome of the race was of interest to all between the wars.'

MOTHERING SUNDAY

'At Stanbridge we picked primroses from the large vicarage garden and made posies for Mothering Sunday.'

MAY DAY

'In our schooldays at the beginning of the century, I think we used to look forward to May Day more than anything. All the children at Cople school voted for the May Queen and they used to practise the dances after school in the village hall. Then on May Day the queen was taken to Ickwell Green on a decorated horse-drawn trolley with her attendants, the last year's queen and the two page boys. The Boy Scout band would march in front and all the dancers had to walk behind. When they got to the green the queen was crowned by her predecessor. People came from miles around, some on bikes and some in horse-drawn carriages. It was about three miles from the farm where we lived and I remember we used to walk there with our mother. After the crowning the dancing started around the maypole. They looked very pretty in their big hats and pretty smocks. They sang as they danced, plaiting the ribbons round the maypole. The older ones who had left school would do Morris dancing. Then there were swinging boats, coconut shies and all the fun of the fair, including sticks of rock which they used to make on the green. Then there was the long walk home but it was well worth it.'

EMPIRE DAY

'Empire Day was always kept at my school in Bedford Road, Kempston, with a girl dressed as Britannia and her courtiers around her. We all had little flags and we sang patriotic songs and waved the flags. I fancied myself as Britannia but I was tall and thin and hardly the type they were looking for.'

FAIRS AND FEASTS

'As a child in the late 1920s to early 1930s I remember the little fair which used to visit Lidlington where I lived. It was called "The Stattie" and was run by a Mr and Mrs Smith.

Mrs Smith, I was given to understand, was a true Romany, with long black hair which was plaited and coiled around her head, like huge ear-phones, and from her ears dangled gold earrings. She wore a longish black skirt, a blouse with sleeves rolled up and a large apron which covered most of her skirt. The things that fascinated me most were her long, black lace-up boots.

My mother used to tell me she too had worn boots like that when she was a little girl.

Mrs Smith is remembered as being exceptionally polite and soft spoken, and when coming to the shop which my parents ran, would wait outside until other customers had completed their purchases. I believe she had married outside her own culture.

Mr Smith attended to the swings with their brightly coloured ropes, and the coconut shy; and I remember a hoop-la stall and a kind of skittles with balls on lengths of cord or elastic. There was also a stall selling the famous "Spit-rock", nicknamed thus because, supposedly, the makers spat on their hands before pulling the candy which was thrown over a large hook, then pulled and twisted and thrown many times more. There were two types, one light brown and the other very dark and shiny, both with lighter stripes. These were eventually cut to the size of large "humbugs", and tasted very good too.

The fair was held on an open space of land by The Green Man public house, and the local children greatly looked forward to its annual visit, as doubtless did others when it came to their local villages.'

'Stevington Feast was held on the Monday and Tuesday after 19th September. The day before was a family Sunday, when families gathered for dinner and tea. The older or married members of the family would give the younger children pennies for spending at the fair on the Monday and Tuesday evenings. At one time the lord of the manor paid for two free rides for every village child.

The Mannings fair would come, the large caravans having to negotiate the Cross and get into the field which is now Burridges Close. One year Mrs Manning gave birth whilst the fair was at Stevington and ever after she gave one free ride to the children to celebrate her child's birthday. People came from miles around to the fair – the girls looked forward to it all year as they hoped they would see their boyfriends there. The Methodists always held their Harvest Festival on that Sunday, followed by the Baptists the next Sunday and the church the following Sunday.'

'The Bedford Regatta was the most popular event in the town before the First World War and Mother was taken there each year. When it was revived in 1919 five friends punted and poled the three miles to Bedford and found a free place to tie up. They were very tired when they had punted the three miles back again in the evening.'

'In the spring a small fair, otherwise known as The Stattie, would arrive and set up in front of the Royal Oak public house at Houghton Conquest. This consisted of four swinging boats, a coconut shy and a sweet and rock stall. The fair lady made the spit-rock, a large iron hook hung down from the stall and over this she would wind the mixture spitting on her hands occasionally until it was the right texture, this done it would be put in a straight line on a board and cut into pieces with scissors. You could also buy a stattie ball made of fine knit cotton and filled with sawdust, with a piece of round elastic attached to it so it bounced up and down.'

'The last week in September was Salford Feast. Two fairs came in the 1930s with their roundabouts, swing boats, shooting ranges, coconut shies, knocking down skittles and various other stalls. Each booth was lit by flaming torches, giving the fields a fairy tale quality. Continuous music was provided by a hurdy gurdy. To us the people seemed to live an enchanted life in their horse-drawn caravans.'

HARVEST HOME

'The church was always dresed up for Harvest Festival at Stevington. The choir had a harvest supper with the vicar, Rev Sproule. Rev Sproule rode round the villages on his bicycle, always in black and wearing breeches. He lived in a large cold vicarage next to Stevington church.'

'This is an old song that was sung at the Harvest Home suppers at Biddenham. Miss Bertha Simmons recorded it on tape at Christmas 1977 – she died in 1979 aged over 90 years. The song dates back some 80 years at least.

O'er England, Scotland, Ireland I've been,
And over the Welsh mountains true beauty have I seen,
But of all the lassies in the West I solemn do declare,
None are so pretty as the girls of Bedfordshire.
They are handsome, charming, dainty and fair, good tempered, brisk and lively,
Red cheeks and jet black hair and the prettiest girls in England are the girls of Bedfordshire.

Some can use the fork and rake, some can drive the plough,
Some can sing like nightingales whilst milking of the cow,
Some can dance the hornpipe whilst going to the fair,
Oh the prettiest girls of England are the girls of Bedfordshire.
They are handsome, charming, etc, etc, etc.

Ye roving men of England if you want to change your life,

Hasten down to Bedfordshire and choose yourself a wife,
And when in happy wedlock joined a toast you will give,
Success to all those girls that in Bedfordshire do live.
They are handsome, charming, etc, etc, etc.'

REMEMBRANCE DAY

'Remembrance, or Armistice, Day was always held on 11th November before the war. Poppies were worn on that day only. They would be purchased for a penny, threepence or sixpence, or a large cluster at two shillings and sixpence for your car.

At school we all assembled in the hall for a service and the two minutes silence, which started with the firing of a gun at the barracks. If it fell on a Saturday I would be in Bedford town and at the firing of the gun all traffic would stop in the High Street and there would be complete silence for two minutes.'

CHRISTMAS

'The children who went to Biddenham church in the morning were invited back to Major Holland Griffiths' house near the church to sing carols in his beautiful hall. They were rewarded with sixpence and an orange each.'

'My father used to go to Carters in Lime Street, a kind of warehouse, and purchase small gifts for our stockings. These consisted of sugar mice and clocks, and oranges were tucked inside and always a *new* penny, and the stockings were hung from the large mantelpiece in the living room of our house in Stevington. Christmas dinner was always a chicken and plum pudding, and mince pies were enjoyed after church in the morning. Then Dad would play games; a man of great patience, he couldn't read or write but was very knowledgeable.'

'We used to hang our stockings up at Christmas time and about all we would get would be a chocolate mouse and an orange; that's all our parents could afford. I wonder what children would say if that was all they got now? When Mother mixed the Christmas pudding she would put in a silver threepenny bit and there would be great excitement at dinner time to see who found it. Then we had one cracker each and a few nuts and that's about all, but we were very happy. Then in the evening we used to sit round the fire and sing carols, and the last thing at night one of us would go out with our father round the sheep yard to see if they were alright, as we often had a lot of lambs at Christmas time. On Boxing Day we always looked forward to a full day's rabbiting!'

Index